P9-DFT-107

In memory of

Trudie Douglas

who created the delightful pen and ink sketches

1907–1995

Vulcan Street

STAIRWAY WALKS
in SAN FRANCISCO

Adah Bakalinsky

Drawings by Trudie Douglas
Maps by Pat Beebee

WILDERNESS PRESS
BERKELEY

Third Edition April 1995
Second printing November 1995
Third printing October 1998

Copyright © 1984, 1992, 1995 by Adah Bakalinsky

Drawings by Trudie Douglas
Maps by Pat Beebee
Cover design by Larry Van Dyke

Library of Congress Card Catalog Number 95-1502
International Standard Book Number 0-89997-184-9

Manufactured in the United States of America

Published by Wilderness Press
2440 Bancroft Way
Berkeley, CA 94704
(510) 843-8080
Write for a free catalog
(800) 443-7227
FAX (510) 548-1355
e-mail *mail@wildernesspress.com*
www.wildernesspress.com

 Recycled paper, 20% post-consumer waste

Library of Congress Cataloging-in-Publication Data
Bakalinsky, Adah.
    Stairway walks in San Francisco / by Adah Bakalinsky ; drawings by
Trudie Douglas ; maps by Pat Beebee. — 3rd ed.
        p.   cm.
    ISBN 0-89997-184-9
    1. San Francisco (Calif.)—Tours. 2. Walking—California—San
Francisco—Guidebooks. 3. Stairs—California—San Francisco—
Guidebooks. I. Title.
    F869.S33B35   1995
    917.94'610453—dc20   95-1502
                                                            CIP

DEDICATION

This book is dedicated to Max, who can make a walk to the grocery store an adventure; to our parents, Morris and Helen Packerman and Joseph and Selma Bakalinsky; to our children, Eric, Polly, Mimi and Alan; and to our grandchildren, Noah, Kieran and Alyssa—all good walkers.

ACKNOWLEDGMENTS

What began as a game—how many stairways can we find, how many steps can we leap over, how fast can we get to the top—gradually became an introduction to city geography and history. When we became more disciplined, the game became a book. The idea of a book came from Judith Lynch, who was coordinator of City Guides, who gives free historical and architectural walks, under the sponsorship of Friends of the San Francisco Public Library. Many members of City Guides, and non-City Guides volunteered their time and services toward the completion of the first Stairway Walks book. I acknowledged them individually in the first (1984) edition. I want to express my gratitude to three people who played important roles in bringing the second (1992) edition to completion: Gene Smith, editor, whose humor and feedback kept me on my toes; Trudie Douglas, artist, whose superb pen-and-ink drawings express her delight (absolutely contagious) in new views of the City; and Pat Beebee, cartographer, whose maps have a special lilt inviting one to join the walk.

I have been privileged to receive criticism and suggestions from the fine urban explorers who have walked my stairway walks; I have been fortunate in finding generous people who inform me about one thing or another pertinent to stairway walking in neighborhoods. I am indebted to many neighborhood activists who have kept me apprised of their progress in beautifying their stairways with thoughtful plantings of trees, shrubs, and flowers. I acknowledged them individually in the 1992 edition.

With each succeeding edition of *Stairway Walks*, I feel I am writing another chapter in a film series. The plot advances, new characters emerge, the scroll of credits becomes longer, and the line of history becomes clearer.

San Francisco has been fortunate to have an organization such as San Francisco Beautiful, a nonprofit, environments gadfly group that provides matching grants for beautification projects to neighborhood groups. Their active stairway committee (I want to thank Tova Wiley for her unflagging devotion to this venture) has accelerated our awareness of stairways as valuable, widely-used pedestrian paths, linking neighborhoods throughout the City.

As my work with San Francisco Beautiful extends into more neighborhoods where residents are trying to beautify the stairways and develop surrounding gardens, my contacts and sources of information increase, and I have the opportunity to see cooperative ideas develop from tentative beginnings to completion. The result is one more pocket of beauty in San Francisco and one more confident community group. I want to give special acknowledgment to Mel Baker of the Department of Public Works, Environmental Street Services. He is EVERY NEIGHBORHOOD'S BEST FRIEND. We call him for debris cleanup, tree trimming, plant materials; he facilitates the installation of water meters; he makes sure we reach the proper city department officials for project assistance; upon request, he will meet with neighborhood groups; and he always has workable suggestions.

In this 1998 printing I want to thank walking friends who have kept me apprised of changes in the neighborhoods and who have scouted the routes and made detailed notes: Jeanne Fisher, Joan Gordon, Ed Griffith, Mike Hayman, Michael Lampen, Joe McNally, Terry Milne, Marilyn Straka, Robbie Straka, and Jay White. A special thanks to Carol Talpers who loves the book.

—*Adah Bakalinsky*

FOREWORD

by Nancy Pease

Every time I see a stairway in San Francisco, I think of Adah Bakalinsky. Like Adah, I love the City's stairways: they are our urban public footpaths that lead us to panoramic views, unique neighborhoods, and special hidden places.

Adah's walks are veritable treasure hunts. She leads the intrepid explorer up and down stairways and along city streets and obscure lanes, pointing out the architectural jewels, the historical gems, and the cultural pearls which make up the city... and lure the readers of *Stairway Walks in San Francisco* on yet another walk.

Try them one by one, "as is", armed with this book. Or, take a Muni map, bus fare, and a few friends, and make a day of it doing two or more walks—perhaps with lunch interspersed—and use Muni to get back to your starting point.

Ever since the first edition of *Stairway Walks In San Francisco* was published in 1984, it has been a "must have" book for people exploring the city on foot. I'm so glad this third edition is now available. Set forth with this book, on these walks, and you'll find yourself knowing the city as you never did before. Thanks Adah!

CONTENTS

Acknowledgments
Foreword *by Nancy Pease*
Contents
Introduction

INTRODUCTION

San Francisco is a "walking city." Built upon forty-two hills, it is surrounded by the Bay on the east, the Pacific on the west, a peninsula on the south, and on the north, the Golden Gate. Within those confines, variety is constant. Light and water combine to produce striking effects on bridges and buildings. The Bank of America at 555 California Street is a scintillating pattern of reflections. San Francisco's weather produces subtle color changes in the sky. Throughout the day this provides a seductive backdrop for signs, unfinished structures, and hills.

The hills accelerate changes in perspective as one walks around corners or circles the ridges. Landmarks recede and suddenly emerge in a landscape abounding in inclines and angled streets. The Mount Sutro TV tower viewed from the mid-Sunset district is a beautiful sky sculpture; from the Sutro area, it looks like a ship in space. From Ashbury Heights, it looks pedestrian. It appears large and within touching distance from the outer Sunset district; walk two blocks toward it, and it is small and oh so far away.

The streets of San Francisco range from flat, such as Irving, to almost vertical like sections of Duboce and Filbert. In fact, the City Fathers and developers found grading the streets a primary obstacle in turning San Francisco from a tent town into a city of timbered houses. Some of the hills were completely demolished in the process; others were cut into without much planning. When the task seemed insurmountable, the "street" ended.

How does one maneuver from one street level to another when there are so many hills? Via stairways, of course! There are more than 350 stairways—crooked, straight, short, long, concrete, wooden, balustraded, or unadorned. Paved streets often follow the contours of hills, but the stairways allow direct vertical access from one street to another. They are a surprise wherever one finds them and they are one of the least celebrated aspects of San Francisco.

Many of the stairways are not easily identified. In some cases, the Structural Engineer's Office may have a name listed but no sign posted. In other cases, the stairway is not officially listed because it is privately maintained. I have named these stairways by referring to the closest cross street.

The 27 walks in the book vary in length and elevation. They are designed for the curious walker. Each walk takes two to two and one-half hours if you enjoy all the sights, scents, and sounds along the way. Pacific Heights, Russian Hill, and other well-known areas are included, but I have focused more attention on neighborhoods that are not usually featured in guidebooks and not well-known to residents of other San Francisco neighborhoods.

The starting points of every walk can be reached by car or by public transportation (call 673-MUNI for information).

Some of the walks are quite strenuous, although I feel the stupendous views and delightful discoveries justify the strain. Buses are available at several points of most walks, and alternate routes are occasionally suggested for specified reasons.

I have found it worthwhile to carry binoculars because the views throughout add to the enjoyment of the walks; a good map; and a compass (optional) to help correlate directions of landmarks.

Five impressions became more distinct as I searched for stairways in San Francisco.

One: San Francisco still has woodsy, unmanicured areas to explore. Thanks to organizations dedicated to keeping San Francisco a beautiful and viable place to live, we have been able to hold on to these tracts; with future legislation friendly to open space, we may yet preserve them.

Two: San Francisco has thousands of views, from panoramic to miniature. Some of the most notable ones, one that visitors should see but usually don't, are in areas secluded by hilly, craggy terrain. An untapped source of changing views is *between* the houses as one walks by.

Three: Our street system appears undisciplined, but I have personally felt that it is a cloned organism with an unusual defense mechanism. For instance: there are streets and alleys and stairways with no visible name; Thomas Bros. maps may list a name that is so obscure, no one has ever heard of it; some streets halve themselves, then appear several blocks later; some streets angle into another; others continue to be listed on maps even though they may be blocked off or terminated.

Four: Both commercial and official maps have inaccuracies. I used several to counter-check my notes because some routes walked differently from the way they looked on the maps.

Five: The city parts fit together. Key streets connect one neighborhood to another, and the hills form a scaffold for the disparate jutting, circular and rectangular areas.

After years of walking in San Francisco, enjoying the ambience, and feeling extremely lucky that I live here, my greatest reward arrived the day I felt the geography of San Francisco indelibly imprinted in my bones and psyche. I use its image as my framework in designing the stairway walks, keeping in mind the corridor streets and stairs that allow us to walk the width and length of the city.

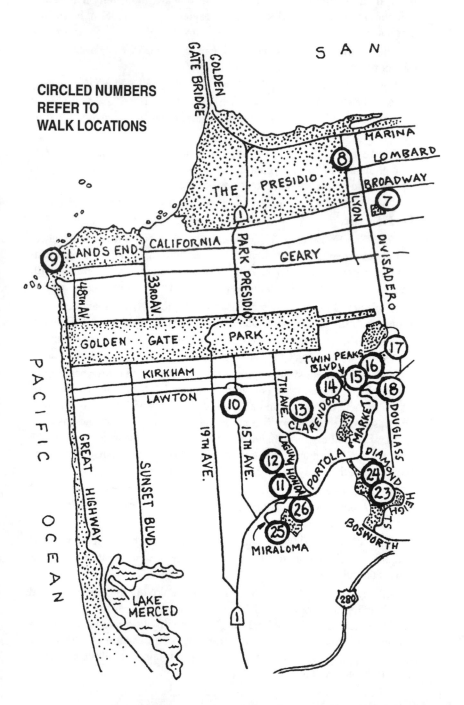

CIRCLED NUMBERS
REFER TO
WALK LOCATIONS

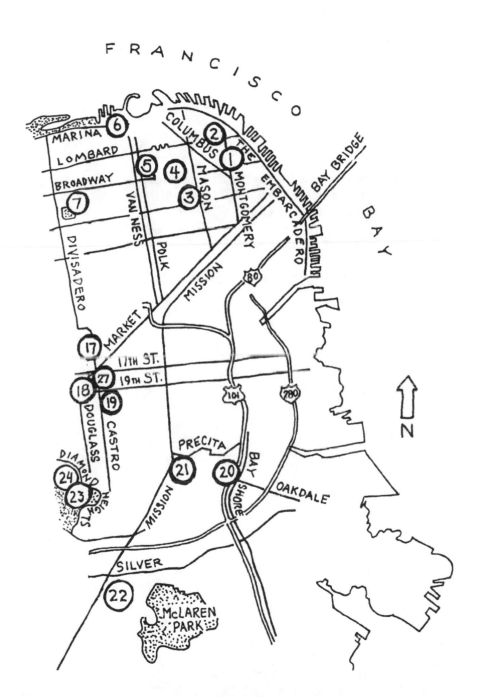

San Francisco is a city that transcends itself.
I have only to mention that I live in San Francisco
to hear the inevitable,

"It's my favorite city,"

or "It is so beautiful,"

or "Oh, you are so lucky."

A.B.

Walk 1

YERBA BUENA
& TELEGRAPH HILL
An Amphibious Walk!

This Amphibious Walk is an adventure in contemporary archeology. It covers fill land where the early commercial life of the City was located: on The Embarcadero and part of the Financial district. It covers the Northeast Waterfront Historic District (from Union to Broadway between Sansome and The Embarcadero), and it covers some of Telegraph Hill.

These areas are my favorite kinds of neighborhoods because they incorporate mixed use. There are well-designed condominiums and restaurants scattered amidst retail stores and service industries. Renovated and remodeled buildings house architects, graphic designers, multi-image labs, and TV studios. There is always foot traffic: the distances are short from one area to another. The atmosphere is electric with the mixture of residents, visitors, restaurant guests, hardy health club members, strollers, and people taking their ease at Levi's Plaza near the fountains or amid the Lombardy poplars in Sydney Walton Park.

Since 1851, San Francisco and surrounding communities have been encroaching on the Bay, filling it to one-third its original size with whatever is conveniently at hand—abandoned ships, garbage, quarry from Rincon and Telegraph Hills—in order to extend piers to accommodate trading ships, and to make room for warehouses.

Conservationists became alarmed by the deleterious ecological effects of this random filling. In 1961, citizens organized the "Save San Francisco Bay Association"; in 1965, state legislation was passed to form the Bay

1

Conservation and Development Commission (BCDC), a permanent agency mandated to plan and regulate long-term use of the Bay.

The Gold Rush to California was the nineteenth-century rite of passage, the Outward Bound of the 1800s. It took all one's ingenuity to survive, in addition to statesmanship, business acumen, and physical stamina. San Francisco, the entry point for people coming overland by wagon, and around the Horn by ship, had a population of approximately 450 at the first census count in 1847; approximately 20,000 by the end of 1849.

Gradually, as more families arrived in the City, social services were organized; schools, libraries and churches were opened; lectures, opera, concerts, readings and theater were offered.

■ We begin at Sansome and Greenwich, walking east on Greenwich to Battery. As we walk closer to the Bay, we can view the Treasure Island

MAP 1

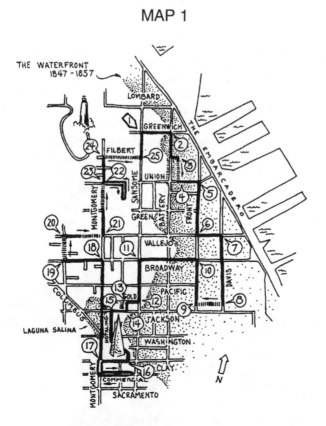

Museum through the fence. Treasure Is. was man-made for the 1939 Golden Gate International Exposition, and at present belongs to the Navy.

■ Right turn on Battery. Fog City Diner across the street contributes to the affability of the street with guests waiting patiently and with good humor for their reservations to be honored. Il Fornaio restaurant, bakery and coffee bar on the northeast section of Levi's Plaza, has an inviting ambience, and always there are people enjoying delectables at any time of day. It is on the site of what was Griffing's Wharf during the Gold Rush, and it was constructed by planking over a sunken hulk. Several sunken ships dating from 1851 are in this area. (The Palmyra is supposed to be underneath the large planter with the pine tree in the center, adjoining the glassed section of Il Fornaio.)

■ The Italian Swiss Colony building, with the lovely arches, adjoins the restaurant on the left, and is one of the original warehouses in this district. The interior contained a well useful in staying a roof fire in 1906.

Walk 1: Yerba Buena & Telegraph Hill Route

Public Transportation: Muni Bus #42 stops here.

1. Begin at Sansome and Greenwich. Walk east on Greenwich to Battery.
2. Right on Battery.
3. Left on Filbert. Walk through courtyard, right to ascend short stairway to Union.
4. Left on Union to Front.
5. Right on Front, past Green to Vallejo.
6. Left on Vallejo.
7. Right on Davis to Sydney Walton Park.
8. Ascend stairway to platform on Jackson. Descend on other side to Front.
9. Right on Front to Broadway.
10. Left on Broadway to Sansome.
11. Left on Sansome to Gold.
12. Right on Gold to Balance.
13. Left on Balance to Jackson.
14. Right on Jackson to Hotaling.
15. Left on Hotaling, cross Washington, walk to Sansome.
16. Right on Clay. Walk through the redwood grove of Transamerica Bldg. Return to Clay to Montgomery.
17. Left on Montgomery to Commercial. Return to walk on Montgomery to Broadway.
18. Left on Broadway to Kearny.
19. Ascend Kearny stairway to Vallejo.
20. Right on Vallejo. Descend stairway to Montgomery.
21. Left to ascend Montgomery Stwy. to Union.
22. Right on Union cul-de-sac to Calhoun cul-de-sac.
23. Return to Montgomery. Right to Filbert.
24. Right to descend Filbert Stwy. to Sansome.
25. Left on Sansome to Greenwich to our beginning.

Levi Strauss & Co. national headquarters is located in this complex, built in 1982. I find the Plaza a most rewarding space to experience—visually, from the Filbert Stwy. or from the parkway; physically, either walking through from one end to another; or sitting on a bench or on a knoll, or near the waterfall. There is an integration of the components that foster a dynamic interchange of people and structures and plantings.

Cross Battery to walk through the park; descend the stairway, following along the right-hand path through the courtyard, where the employees' fitness center is. The granite planters filled with primula along the walk are very attractive.

We take the stairs to Union. At the corner to our right is the old Ice House (built 1914, remodeled 1970 for use as wholesale showrooms for interior decorators); now the building is used for offices.

Turn left on Union. The three- and four-story brick structures on the street, part of the historic warehouse district, were formerly a cooperage, Whittier Fuller Paint Co., the Union Warehouse, American Sugar Refinery; now they are converted to spaces for architects, interior designers and communication sales.

Right on Front. Part of the Coast walk follows along this section of The Embarcadero, and on weekends The Embarcadero is alive with bicyclists, joggers, walkers and skateboarders.

Cross Green St. This block between Front and Battery was the location of the Cunningham warehouses during the Gold Rush period. Look to the right to the top of the east slope of Telegraph Hill. Jagged, mostly sandstone and shale, it was quarried by the Gray Bros., who were finally stopped from excavating when the terrible rock slide of 1923 occurred.

Continue to Vallejo. In 1854, piles were driven almost 40 feet through fill and sand down to bedrock for the foundation of the Pelican Paper Warehouse on the northwest corner. We turn left and then right on Davis for a clear view of the Bay.

We continue on Davis and walk through Sydney Walton Park, a two-acre greenspace dedicated in 1965. Walton (1901–1960), was vice-chairman of the San Francisco Redevelopment Agency, and was responsible for the concept of the Golden Gateway Center. The produce market was formerly located here; now, it is at Bayshore and Alemany.

■ Several sculptures are in the park. The bronze one, "Portrait of Georgia O'Keeffe" by Marisol, is startling because her hands are detached from the rest of her body. One hand grips a staff, and the other is at rest; meanwhile, her eyes embrace everything that goes on in front of her. Two dogs are by her side. I personally like this non-heroic style of sculpture portraits. There are several other sculptures to enjoy, including a stabile by George Rickey.

■ We walk up the stairway to the platform on Jackson that leads to Golden Gateway apartments, and onto the Embarcadero complex, and descend, going west on Jackson. (If you want to take a detour into the Embarcadero Center, I would suggest you leave it for the end of the walk.) The Embarcadero is one of my favorite art galleries because it is always open, and I am very fond of the sculptures. One percent of the cost of the buildings is mandated for art works.

■ Look over Walton Park, the Lombardy poplars, the people enjoying their lunches, the fine circle of the Golden Gateway condos and small retail stores along the sunken walkway, and if you're in luck, the wild parrots in the trees.

■ Walking on Jackson, we immediately sense the ambience of a village—a particular, personal shopping center, with a large grocery market, a variety of lunch and custom-sandwich places, a drug store, a theater and restaurants. The customers are known to the clerks; everything is within walking distance. It's so civilized.

■ Turn right on Front. (If you would like to walk a block or more farther on Jackson—for food or ambience—do so, then come back to Front.) Continue to Broadway and turn left.

■ The plaque at No. 100 Broadway commemorates the building of the first wharf in 1847 by William Clark. The plaque on the side of #120 Broadway commemorates the landing of the ship, Brooklyn, in 1846. Three hundred Mormon colonists arrived here under the leadership of Samuel Brannan. He brought his printing press in the hold of the ship and founded the STAR, the first newspaper in San Francisco. His office was at No. 743 Washington St. For many years the Mormon Church officials persisted in hounding Brannan for money they said he owed. He eluded them; when told that the money was for God and the Church, he declared if God wants him to give the money He would have to ask for it.

■ At Sansome, we turn left, then right on Gold, one of the numerous alleys in this part of the City, then left on Balance, named for the sunken ship that lies at Front and Jackson.

■ We cross Jackson, and walk in Hotaling Alley, named for A.P. Hotaling's famed saloon and distillery (No. 429 Jackson). It withstood the fire and earthquake of 1906 along with the other buildings in the 400 block.

■ We cross Washington St., and turn left, and then right on Sansome. At the corner of Clay, No. 509 was the Niantic Bldg., named for the abandoned ship that provided one side of the structure. The Niantic was deserted by its crew in 1849 and was converted into a hotel. Continue right on Clay, and walk through the Redwood Grove established by Transamerica for its employees and the general public. It's a popular lunch place, and during the summer there are live concerts at the noon hour. We particularly like the sculpture by Glenna Goodacre, of a group of six children whose movements are caught in mid-air and expressed with great joy and abandon—jumping rope, skipping and hopping. One day we saw a young man join the children at the end of the line in a similar pose. He requested a portrait taken of all of them. I was pleased to comply. The Transamerica has art exhibits in the lobby which I recommend seeing.

■ The original building on this site was the 1853 Montgomery Block, affectionately known as the Monkey Block. Built by Henry Halleck, it was also known as Halleck's Folly because he spent $2 million dollars for it. Four stories high, it had a fish market, grocery and the Saloon Bank Exchange Bar, where one could learn about the best opportunities for investments. In later years law offices and the largest law library in the area were located in the Block. Sun Yat-sen, founder of the Chinese Nationalist movement, had his office here during his exile, around 1911. In the 1920s and 1930s, artists, writers and dancers rented studio/living quarters here. The rent was affordable, and the camaraderie was legendary. The Monkey Block withstood the 1906 earthquake, but was torn down in 1954 for a parking lot. The Transamerica was built in 1972. The base of Transamerica Pyramid looks terribly heavy, but I like the pyramid shape of the building because as it grows upward it uses less and less space. (If you are inclined, you may ascend the elevator to the 17th floor for a view.)

■ Continue on Clay to Montgomery, and turn left to Commercial to stand in the place where Captain Montgomery sailed up in his ship, the USS Portsmouth, in 1846 to claim Yerba Buena for the U.S.A. The Mexican government acceded. At the end of the narrow street we see Portsmouth Square, now the heart of Chinatown, but formerly the heart of Yerba Buena. (There were many hotels and theaters in this area during the 1850s—the Jenny Lind, the Phoenix, the Adelphi, the Italian Theater and the Chinese Theaters were the better-known.)

■ Turn right on Montgomery. The artifacts from the Niantic, found during excavation of the Pyramid site, are displayed in cases in the lobby

Filbert Street

of the Washington Towers at No. 655 Montgomery. You are welcome to go in.

■ At No. 498, the corner of Jackson, we pass by the old Sherman Bank of 1853 with its triangular doorway (saloons used these swing doors). A visible, readable plaque is on the wall.

■ During the Gold Rush, Jackson and Montgomery was the center of Little Chile. Chilenos, expert at using the Chile wheel to crush gold bearing ore, had come to work in the gold mines. The Sydney Ducks—the Australian convict contingent—lived nearby, and the Hounds—a group of New York toughs—lived around Grant and Pacific. The latter two groups were hate groups intent on eradicating people from Central and South America. Finally, after a particularly vengeful foray into Little Chile, the Vigilante group of 1851, (who called themselves the Law and Order Party), was formed under Sam Brannan's leadership to combat the plundering and marauding of the Hounds and Ducks.

■ The William Stout Architectural bookstore at No. 804 Montgomery is one of the most complete in the country, and one in which I love to browse.

■ Continue to Broadway. At the corner of Montgomery is the On Lok organization's Adult Senior Health Services center and 35 apartments for low income elderly. Seniors are brought by van, and stay for the day to receive health and personal care and the mid-day meal. They participate in social and recreation activities, and are returned home in the evening. One of the exciting programs is the ongoing, intergenerational garden, shared by the frail elderly and about 24 children, ages two to five, of the Child Care program. The garden, transformed from an abandoned cement playground by the San Francisco League of Urban Gardeners, was additionally funded by several groups, among them, San Francisco Beautiful.

■ Turn left to Kearny, then right to ascend the sidewalk stairway. The Edwardian homes on the odd-numbered side are run-down and every time I walk here, I expect them to be gone, and apartments or condos put up in their place. Underneath the street paving we can see remains of the former cobblestone surface.

■ Turn right on Vallejo. We look back to the west to see Russian Hill and the stairway leading up to the Vallejo Terrace (Walk 4). Looking forward to the east, we come to the house No. 448-B Vallejo. It was here that Madame Luisa Tetrazzini (1871–1940), the famous Italian opera soprano, while out walking, (she was on tour in San Francisco), heard the young—12 or 13 years of age—Lena Pagliughi (born 1910), singing. Tetrazzini told Lena's parents she wanted to take their daughter to Italy to teach her opera, and to help launch her career as the second Madame Tetrazzini. The parents refused, but four years later, Lena did travel to

Italy to begin her vocal studies under the direction of Tetrazzini. She subsequently had a long career with the Metropolitan Opera.

■ Walk down the Vallejo Stwy., designed by the Department of Public Works. The Department of Urban Forestry planted the trees and shrubs and maintains them. Many of the residents around the stairway are in their 70s and 80s, and we all attribute their longevity to their daily stairway-walking.

■ Turn left on Montgomery to ascend the stairway to Union. Turn right into the Union cul-de-sac, then right into Calhoun. Some of the oldest houses in San Francisco are in this block. Nos. 291, 291-A, and 287 were built in the 1860s. The high retaining wall at the end of the street was built during the Works Progress Administration in 1939.

■ Return to Montgomery and turn right. We stop for a moment in the middle of the street to look at No. 1360. The exterior is in the shape of a ship, complete with a ship-like upper deck. Etched into the glass over the central entrance are a gazelle, palm trees, and ocean waves. The sgraffito panels on the side of the Art Moderne apartment house shows The Worker holding the globe of the world above the Bay Bridge. The bridge towers on the panel are repeated by the actual Bay Bridge towers just beyond it. What extraordinary planning! It trumps *trompe l'oeil*. Actually, the apartment house is more famous as the setting of the Humphrey Bogart/Lauren Bacall film, *Dark Passage*, a 1947 movie.

■ Before descending the historic Filbert Stwy., walk over to see the mural on the retaining wall across the street. A resident commissioned the mural of Ginger, an apricot-colored teacup poodle. Dick Fosselman and Rick Helf, the artists, cleverly incorporated the real water hydrant into the scene. A little garden spot was designed next to the mural. Since all this has been in place, the area is free from garbage and other blight, while being a source of humor.

■ A plaque on the Filbert stairs says: "Filbert Steps, Darrell Place, Napier Lane. In appreciation of Grace Marchant for unselfish, devoted energy in the beautification of Filbert Gardens." The late Grace Marchant moved to Filbert Steps in 1950, when the area was a dumping ground 30 feet deep. The city gave her permission to burn the dump, and it burned— for three days straight. Thirty years she labored on the stairway gardens, which were dedicated to her on May 4, 1980. Marchant died in 1982 at the age of 96. The gardens are cared for by her neighbor, friend and protege; the city contributes water for maintenance.

■ Darrell Pl. and Napier Ln. are "paper streets." They appear as streets on maps and in street guides, but Darrell is more like a trail, and Napier consists only of 12-foot wooden planks, and Filbert, through the gardens, is a wooden stairway—shades of ghost towns left over from Gold Rush days.

Fire is always a hazard, and in these areas where there is no room for trucks, the Fire Department stores equipment as inconspicuously as possible. Next to the blue fire hydrants on the walkway (blue is the code for connection to a high-pressure system) is a storage box for two small fire hydrants and a hose.

An undulating walkway planted with rosebushes leads to No. 273 Filbert; the earliest request for water hookup for No. 267 was in January 1873.

The Gothic cottage at No. 228 (1873) was used as a grocery store. Next door, No. 226, is a renovated miner's shack from 1863.

The lower part of Filbert Stwy. is concrete; many of the wild nasturtiums, fennel and blackberries, once profuse along the sides of the hill, have been cut down. But still, the contrast of foliage and the monolithic craggy hill is startling to behold.

As we descend to Sansome St., we are invited forward by the patterned-aggregate plaza walk of Levi's Plaza. The landscaping design by Lawrence Halprin Associates called for granite and trees to simulate the Sierras where Levi Strauss began his career in 1851. He supplied miners with heavy duck cloth pants, reinforced with copper rivets, to withstand tearing from the pull of tools. The cloth was de Nimes serge, from Nimes, France—hence, denim.

The complex, of glass and red brick (to blend with neighboring landmarks), with open steel and glass corridors, consists of five buildings extending from Sansome to Battery and The Embarcadero. Shadows and reflections make the whole complex sparkle. Adding to the self-sufficiency of the environment, and to the amenities for the 3,000 employees, are ancillary services on the lower level. Hellmuth, Obata & Kassabaum were the architects.

We continue on Sansome to Greenwich to our beginning.

Walk 2

TELEGRAPH HILL
& NORTH BEACH
Hills and Fills

We begin our walk in an historic area of North Beach at the intersection of Mason and Bay. During the Gold Rush days, North Beach did extend to the water line near Francisco St. Henry Meiggs, a New York lumberman, built one of the first wharfs into the Bay (between Mason and Powell), built a sawmill, and established a thriving lumber trade (imports from Oregon). He was genial, well-liked, a co-founder of the San Francisco Philharmonic Society, knew politicians and power brokers, and invested heavily in real estate in North Beach and farther west, believing that this area would develop rapidly. He was wrong. He found himself in the untenable position of being personally bankrupt, and, since he had embezzled City funds, responsible for a financial crisis in San Francisco. Banks closed, many permanently, and investors lost their savings. In 1854, "Honest Harry" Meiggs managed to sail away to Chile; he made another fortune building a railroad through the mountains to Peru. He repaid most of his San Francisco debts, and died in Lima in 1877, having been denied return to California.

During the 1850s, the North Beach waterfront was a dynamic community. Conditions were in flux—there were so many people coming in—emigrants from the east, immigrants from overseas; some in transit, some to settle here.

Supportive services were established—the fishing boats, the breweries, the forges, the slaughterhouses; there were restaurants and saloons, import stores and hostelries.

The 1906 earthquake leveled everything in this quarter except the Ferry Building, which at that time was the tallest structure in San Francisco. The area was soon rebuilt, and the City celebrated its rebirth with the Panama-Pacific International Exposition of 1915.

Over the years, the San Francisco port has diminished in importance. The thrust of the Port Authority's master plan is to balance maritime needs and the needs of the public. One of the plans for Fisherman's Wharf is to centralize the fish wholesalers in

MAP 2

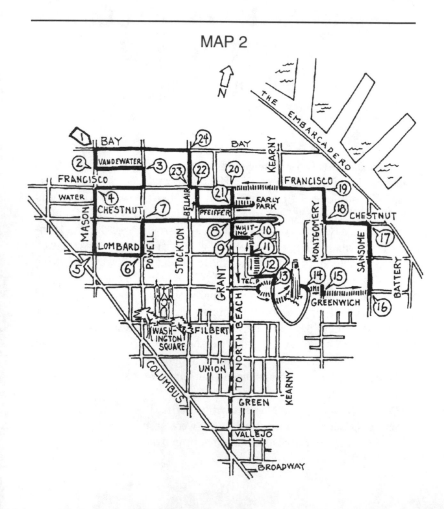

one facility, and return the area to its original purpose—catching, preparing and selling fish to residents and tourists alike.

Along the Embarcadero, the Esplanade at Pier 7 is already functioning as a lovely site for walking, fishing and picnicking; containerization of cargo goes on at Piers 80–96.

■ From the intersection of Mason and Bay, we walk south on Mason, and turn left on Vandewater St., a charming "twitton," as the British call it, softened by trees, and housing many architect and designer offices. Go to the end and turn right on Powell, and right on Francisco to see the Historical Site at No. 407. Until 1980, this was the Bauer-Schweitzer Malt

---

WALK 2: Telegraph Hill/North Beach Route

Public Transportation: Cable Car to Bay and Taylor. Walk one block; Muni Bus #39 to Bay and Mason; #30 to Bay and Leavenworth. Walk three blocks.

1. Begin at Mason and Bay.
2. Left on Vandewater.
3. Right on Powell. Right on Francisco.
4. Left on Mason to Lombard.
5. Left on Lombard to Powell.
6. Left on Powell to Chestnut.
7. Right on Chestnut cul-de-sac. Return to Grant.
8. Left on Grant to Whiting.
9. Left on Whiting St.
10. Right, across from No. 3, up Julius St. Stwy.
11. Walk to Lombard. Next to No. 383, ascend stairway to Telegraph Place.
12. Left on Telegraph Pl. to Telegraph Hill Blvd.
13. Right on Telegraph Hill Blvd. Two doors away from No. 201 descend stairway into cul-de-sac of Greenwich (400 block). Walk around planting area to the left; ascend stairway to Telegraph Hill Blvd. Cross Blvd to ascend stone stairway up the hill toward Coit Tower. Follow footpath that veers to the left and then toward the right side of the Tower.
14. Come around the front of the building, then bear right to cross the Blvd., and descend the Greenwich Stwy. to Montgomery.
15. Cross Montgomery, bear right to continue down Greenwich Stwy.
16. Left on Sansome to Chestnut.
17. Left on Chestnut to Montgomery.
18. Right on Montgomery to Francisco.
19. Left on Francisco. Ascend stairway to Grant.
20. Left on Grant to ascend stairway to Jack Early Park on left side of street.
21. Return to Grant and cross the street to walk through Pfeiffer St. to Bellair Pl. to Francisco.
22. Left on Francisco to Stockton.
23. Right on Stockton to Bay.
24. Left on Bay to Mason to our beginning.

Company, the last barrel-malting factory west of the Mississippi. Their high-quality malt was sold to small American breweries such as Anchor, and was also exported to Japan. When it became economically infeasible to continue operations, the building was sold and is currently being renovated for condominiums.

■ Left turn on Mason. A mural of aquatic life embellishes the gymnasium wall adjoining the North Beach playground and pool. We make a left on Lombard. No. 660, the Telegraph Hill Neighborhood Center, has been in existence since 1890. Nonsectarian and privately supported, it was begun by two wealthy women (influenced by Jane Addams of Hull House in Chicago) to provide services to immigrants from Europe. The present program includes health and educational services to new immigrants from the Orient, to seniors and to children, pre-school and older. Flower beds provide an inviting entrance, and in the back is a vegetable garden. Turn left on Powell and right on Chestnut.

■ Two blocks down, at the intersection of Grant Ave. and Chestnut, we have a long view of Marin toward the north and west. We see the boats anchored at Fisherman's Wharf, we see Piers 33 and 35, and a container ship proceeding toward the Oakland port. Farther in the distance is Pier 39, well-known for its fine horticultural displays of container-flowers; for a colony of sea lions that have taken up residence along the wharf; good restaurants; and friendly stores. The outdoor spaces encourage strolling, and the area is very popular with young people and children. It's a great place to watch fireworks on July 4. I feel these are important enough reasons to lessen my negative reaction to the architecture. Angel Island State Park is to the north.

■ No. 298 Chestnut is a Mediterranean-type home built in 1929. Its tile roof, marble entry, and ceramic Della Robbia plaque are visible through iron gates. We walk to the cul-de-sac end along the left-hand side (designated as Open Space) to obtain a view of the "lowlands", and return to Grant.

■ At Grant Ave. we turn left (south), and left again into Whiting St. cul-de-sac. 3/4 of the block in and to the right, we ascend the nine steps of Julius Alley Stwy; walk to the end, which brings us to Lombard Street. To the left of No. 383 is the short Child St. Stwy. Walk up to Telegraph Pl.; turn left (No. 69 is a charming Japanese-inspired home) to Telegraph Hill Blvd., then turn right.

■ Next to No. 201, we descend a stairway into Greenwich St. cul-de-sac. We circle around the garden area that has been planted (except for the trees) and conscientiously cared for by a neighboring home owner, and walk up the opposite stairway to Telegraph Hill Blvd.

Greenwich Street

■ Cross the Blvd. to ascend the stone stairway leading to the top of Telegraph Hill, once known as Pioneer Park, and then Signal Hill, when the arrival of ships would be signaled from the top to be seen throughout the City. In the 1880s, a restaurant was the chief attraction on the hill, but it burned.

■ Bear right on the footpath that goes toward and around the back of Coit Tower, veering to the left, and then right. Coit Tower, a universally-recognized symbol of the city, was designed by Arthur Brown, Jr. (City Hall) and dedicated in 1933 to the Knickerbocker Engine Company No. 5, one of the San Francisco volunteer fire fighting companies. It was funded by Lillie Hitchcock Coit, who, as a small child, loved to follow No. 5, and became their mascot. The tower rises 179 feet from the crest of Telegraph Hill, itself 284 feet high.

■ We turn right on the redwood-bark path and sit down on the bench for a view of the graceful 1895 Ferry Building and its famous clock. (Lit at night, it is a cameo, a Cinderella, surpassing all other commercial buildings in its delicate beauty.) Construction of three new stairways leading to Coit Tower, a terrace lawn overlooking the Bay, and ramp access, began in Spring, 1998. The tall slender Embarcadero Buildings to the southeast are on the site of the old wholesale-produce market. Because Embarcadero Center is on Redevelopment land and Federal funds partially defrayed building costs, the developer was obliged to spend one percent of the total cost of the project on art works. This resulted in purchases of excellent sculpture and woven hangings that are placed throughout the Center. Directly in front of us is the Transamerica Pyramid; the 48-story dark carnelian granite building is the Bank of America Office Building.

■ As we walk along the right side of Coit Tower, we can look inside and see WPA murals from the 1930s. Intermittent vandalism and/or damage from water seepage has necessitated closing the mural rooms to visitors from time to time. The elevator ride to the top floor is available to the public at a nominal charge. The parking lot has coin telescopes to bring Marin and the East Bay into closeup view .

■ We walk down the front stairs of the Tower and proceed on the footpath to the right; cross Telegraph Hill Blvd. to the continuation of the Greenwich St. Stwy. Descend. This brick section curves, allowing room on each side for wide, terraced, private gardens, behind which the rooftops peek out. The lane running at right angles from No. 356 Greenwich has no name. It connects with the Filbert Stwy. farther south (Walk 1).

■ The first landing of these 147 stairs leads down to Montgomery cul-de-sac and the famous Julius' Castle restaurant, built in 1923. A beautiful, mature fig tree graces the entrance.

■ The lower retaining wall is designed in a random pattern of brick with protruding stones, which is extremely photogenic, so I always remember to look back before I descend the next series of stairs.

■ Cross Montgomery (comparable to an opera singer taking a deep breath) and bear right to the Greenwich sign. Descend the concrete stairs and extended walkways. Along the way we see a cistern for fire fighting, and, on the left side of the walkway, trees (a magnificent magnolia), gardens (roses and irises, ferns and fuschias). The flock of wild parrots obtain sustenance from the juniper berries and loquats near No. 243 where they augment their diet with seeds provided by the hill guardian of the 39 member flock. A beautiful, purple princess tree dominates the garden across from No. 237; a huge, and dramatic-looking pepper tree has accommodated itself to its site at No. 231A.

A tall Deodar cedar tree and a redwood tree in the canyon, provide homes for families of birds. Nasturtiums and invasive fennel usually line the hillsides. In season, blackberries are for the picking. At the foot of the steps, we turn left on Sansome Street and continue north.

The slope of Telegraph Hill, now barely seen from Sansome and Lombard, since the Lombard Plaza apartments were built in 1991, was the amphitheater for the 1996 Janice Joplin rock concert. The bandstand was placed against the cliff, the audience (1,000s) sat informally on the hillside. During intermission, people ambled into Synanon (now the health club at the corner of Montgomery and Chestnut), to buy art works and refreshments.

■ Turn left on Chestnut. A three-story brick building is angled across the corner of Montgomery. Originally built in the late 1800s, it was reconstructed in 1973. We turn right on Montgomery and left on Francisco.

■ At Kearny we walk into the well-cared-for courtyard of the Wharf Plaza subsidized housing for seniors. The gardens provide a delightful place to sit and lunch or visit. The gingko trees are ringed in gold leaves in September. Ascend the well-designed stairway that has a long, elevated walkway (perfect for a dance performance), to the Francisco cul-de-sac. The condos, Telegraph Terrace, are low, and fit into the terrain beautifully.

Turn left on Grant, and in the middle of the next block, left again, to walk up the stairs to Jack Early Park, begun in 1962. It's an unexpected bonus—perfect for views, solitude, and moon-watching.

Come back down, cross Grant, and walk through Pfeiffer Alley, a right-of-way that has become a charming enclave. No. 139–141 dates from 1910, and No. 152, from 1891.

■ Right turn into Bellair Pl. and left on Francisco. Cross the street to see the little cottage at No. 276 which dates from 1863. Delicious aromas surround No. 271, now a cooking school.

■ Continue west on Francisco to Stockton. Turn right to Bay, and left to our beginning.

■ If you wish to explore further for food or sundry items, you have choices available from all compass points, within comfortable walking distances.

■ If you want to explore more of North Beach, walk south on Grant into the upper Grant area for coffee houses and restaurants, and the ambience of resident walkers. The Oriental restaurants plus the poultry and fish and vegetable markets of Chinatown where residents shop, are one block west,on Stockton. The Cost Plus import store at No. 2552 Taylor is a popular place to buy inexpensive, imported trinkets, foods and housewares. Six blocks west, at the foot of Columbus, is The Cannery, at No. 2801 Leavenworth, an unusual shopping complex; two blocks beyond is Ghirardelli Square, another historic setting for specialty shops (Walk 6).

Walk 3

NOB HILL
Castles in the Air

Nob Hill, 376 feet above the Bay, is wedged between Pacific Heights to the west, Russian Hill toward the north, and North Beach and Chinatown to the east. Millions of tourists have traversed Nob Hill on the cable cars, gliding both north-south on Powell St. between Market St. and Fisherman's Wharf and east-west on California St.

An irony of this walk is that the most interesting characteristics can actually be noted by standing still—looking up to appreciate the architectural details high on the buildings and looking from eye level to enjoy the delight of the cable car riders. Binoculars can add extended range to our sightings.

Nob Hill is famous for the views, luxury hotels and apartment houses which we see on our walk. The only "neighbors" we see on this area of our tour may be doormen, or hotel guests alighting from a taxi—or the elderly rich assisted by nurses or companions. But there is a neighborhood, and in the side streets and charming alley ways we find "talking" neighbors to visit with, and gardening neighbors who share cuttings. The Nob Hill Association, the neighborhood watchdog organization founded in 1923, is actively concerned with the environment and community issues.

■ We begin at California and Leavenworth on the crest of Nob Hill. We walk north on Leavenworth on the odd-numbered side for a few yards and turn left into Acorn, one of San Francisco's most attractive, viable alleys, full of plants and color. The inviting green walkway, clay pots full of flowers ringed around an utility pole, plus bedding plants and raised beds

19

of flowers are the work of two neighbors who have cared for the alley for many years.

■ From Acorn, we turn north on Leavenworth to Sacramento St. No. 1409 Sacramento is a large building in the Craftsman style.

■ Turn right on Sacramento and walk on the odd-numbered side. The corner building at No. 1202–1206 Leavenworth is a 1910 Julia Morgan design of shingle and stucco, now beautifully covered with vines. The foliage of the street trees adds a softness that makes this section of Sacramento St. very enticing.

■ Turn right into Golden Ct. On both sides of the walkway are rows of tall fuschias. They are a favorite plant of a resident who tends them devotedly. He has discouraged pilfering of the plants by posting a sign: "These fuschias are sprayed weekly with a systemic poison. Systemic means to you that when you touch the plants, the poison goes directly to your bloodstream and then throughout the body. Blindness and facial paralysis result." The fronts of the houses on Golden Ct. face either Leavenworth or Leroy. The grey asbestos sided house on our right was built by the owner in 1950 (the address is officially No. 1154 Leavenworth) on the only empty lot on the street, the original house having been demolished by the 1906 earthquake. He planted the attilio tree in 1947 from a seedling his mother brought in her purse from Italy. Golden Ct. is a special enclave, as is LeRoy, our next right turn, off Sacramento. Two symmetrical rows of plane trees frame the walk which ends with an accent

MAP 3

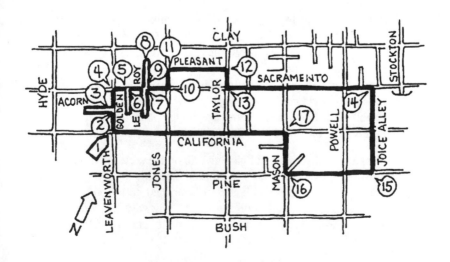

of terra cotta balusters. No. 16 Leroy has very attractive bowed windows. Go across the street into the continuation of Leroy. Here lemon bottlebrush trees on one side and plane trees on the other enhance the short alley. A basilica-shaped structure at the end of the street is the back of No. 1239 Jones St., the Tank High Pressure System of the Fire Department.

■ We walk out of the cul-de-sac, and make a left turn on Sacramento. No. 1325–1323 is a two-flat Victorian; the owner has lived there since 1930. Continue to Jones and turn left.

■ Grace Episcopal Cathedral School for Boys is on the corner of the square block that includes the Diocesan house and the Cathedral itself. The school was built in 1966 for grades kindergarten through eighth.

■ No. 1221 Jones is a luxury apartment and Le Club, at No. 1250 is a restaurant and nightclub. The Comstock Apartments at No. 1333 is named for the Nevada silver lode where James Fair and James Flood, two bonanza kings who lived on Nob Hill, made their fortunes.

■ At the intersection of Pleasant, turn right. Trees are missing, but everything is very clean. A new structure at No. 75 Pleasant has extravagantly large north-facing windows. Some of the basement-skylight glass in the sidewalk at No. 16 is purple with age.

■ We make a right turn on Taylor to go south. No. 1110 is the smallest structure on the block. A one-story, modified three-window bay, it was originally built by James Flood for his coachman.

WALK 3: Nob Hill Route

Public Transportation: Muni Bus #27 goes on Leavenworth; Cable Car goes on California.

1. Begin at California and Leavenworth. North on Leavenworth to Acorn.
2. Left on Acorn. Return to Leavenworth.
3. Left on Leavenworth to Sacramento.
4. Right on Sacramento to Golden.
5. Right on Golden. Return to Sacramento.
6. Right on Sacramento to Leroy.
7. Right on Leroy. Return to Sacramento.
8. Left on Leroy. Return to Sacramento.
9. Left on Sacramento to Jones.
10. Left on Jones to Pleasant.
11. Right on Pleasant to Taylor.
12. Right on Taylor to Sacramento.
13. Left on Sacramento to Joice.
14. Right on Joice Alley, descend stairway to Pine.
15. Right on Pine to Mason.
16. Right on Mason to California.
17. Left on California to our beginning.

Turn left on Sacramento. In the sidewalk in front of No. 1162 Sacramento is a survey monument with the precise latitude and longitude of this spot on the globe inscribed under its cover.

Huntington Park, across the street, is an oasis of inviting benches, plantings, fountains and sculpture, plus a large sandbox, slides and swings for the youngsters. It was donated to the City in 1915 by Mrs. Collis P. Huntington, whose husband, one of the Big Four railroad barons, built his mansion on Nob Hill. The Nob Hill Association, in conjunction with Friends of Recreation and Parks, financed a recent renovation of the park, and has undertaken the responsibility for maintaining it.

As we go along, the back of the landmark Pacific Union Club, one of the most exclusive men's clubs in the country, comes into view. James Flood built this brownstone building as his residence in 1886. Its exterior survived the quake and fire of 1906. In 1912, it was reconstructed and remodeled by Willis Polk. Legend has it that the bronze fence surrounding the property was once the full-time job of a maintenance man.

We also see the white granite Fairmont Hotel. It was readied for its grand opening in 1906, when, on April 18 at 5:15 a.m. the interior was destroyed by the fire (caused by the earthquake) but luckily, the fire insurance didn't expire until midnight! The steel frame survived, and a year later the hotel opened for business. The square block on which it stands was owned by James Fair, Flood's Comstock partner. A contemporary feature of the Fairmont is the exterior elevator, providing an unusual kinetic experience as one gradually ascends while watching the cityscape.

Continue east on Sacramento. No. 1000 Mason is the elegant Brocklebank Apartments, built in 1924. Ornate mythological beasts are positioned atop the entrance.

Down the hill, at No. 920 Sacramento at Joice, is the Donaldina Cameron House, formerly the Chinese Presbyterian Mission Home. The Mission began efforts in 1874 to rescue young Chinese girls brought to San Francisco as factory slaves and prostitutes. Ms. Cameron joined the group in 1895 and continued her missionary work for 40 years. Cameron House currently provides community recreational and social services. The clinker-brick structure was built in 1881, then rebuilt in 1907 by Julia Morgan. Morgan worked in the Bay Area from about 1905 to the 1930s, designing Craftsman-style homes and also elegant structures such as the Hearst Castle at San Simeon.

Cross Sacramento and walk into Joice Alley. Continue in the right-of-way, cross California St., and ahead of us at No. 845 is an Art Deco apartment house, pleasingly symmetrical, with a marble entrance and light standards. Looking toward our right, we see the octagonal green-and-white, electronically-operated traffic control tower for the cable car system at California and Powell. We continue on Joice, arrive at Joice Stwy., and descend. A small shrine to St. Francis is on the landing near the graceful curve of the stairs at Pine. The flats at Nos. 738, 740 and 742 Pine are built in the Pueblo style. Across the street is Monroe Alley, now renamed Dashiell Hammett St.

■ We turn right on Pine. Above the high parapet in back of the Stanford Court Hotel is a cast-stone penguin by Beniamino Bufano, the impecunious artist and bohemian who captured the imagination of San Franciscans and, more important, the financial support of patrons. At the time of his death in 1970, many of his works were stored in warehouses. Until the Bufano Sculpture Park is established, the works are positioned in several places: in the courtyard of the Academy of Sciences; in the North Terminal at the Airport; at the Phelan St. entrance to the Administration Building at San Francisco City College; in the Ordway Building lobby in Oakland; and at Ft. Mason (Walk 6). The Mansion Hotel at No. 2220 Sacramento has a large collection.

■ We are now walking along the original granite retaining wall of the Stanford mansion, which was destroyed by the earthquake. The blocked entrance in the wall may have been for tradesmen. The tower with the finial marks the division between the Stanford and Hopkins properties.

■ Turn right on Mason and walk uphill on the even numbered side. A graduated series of town houses, Nos. 831 to 849, designed by Willis Polk around 1918, provides a delightful counterfoil to the sumptuous structures on the hill.

■ As our bird's-eye view from the top—California St. between Mason and Taylor—comes into focus, we see lines of formidable structures. The inner line of defense (yes, we did feel like Napoleon viewing his fortifications) consists of Hotels Fairmont, Mark Hopkins, Huntington and the Pacific Union Club. The Powell flank is held by the Stanford Court Hotel, with Grace Cathedral and the Cathedral Apartments on the Jones St. side. The secondary defense on Sacramento St. consists of luxury apartments.

■ Standing on the summit, and looking at the details of the Mark Hopkins Hotel and the Fairmont Hotel across the street, we can't help imagining what these buildings would look like with no ornamentation, or built of redwood or corrugated cardboard.

■ We turn left on California. No. 1001, the Morsehead apartments built in 1915, is one of our favorite buildings on the hill. Behind the terra cotta columns and facade are 10 apartments, each 2,000 to 3,000 square feet. The building feels cozier than many on the block. Another of our favorite Nob Hill buildings is No. 1021, a single-family dwelling, with ornate wrought-iron double doors, French doors on the second story, and cut-lace coverings on the windows and glass doors. The Crocker garage next to it is scheduled to be replaced by a new Crocker Hotel. No. 1075 California is the Huntington Hotel, considered by many to be one of the most elegant hotels in the City.

■ We pass the California St. entrance to Huntington Park. From the Taylor St. side of the park, we face the rose-windowed facade of Grace Cathedral. When their current $11 million construction plan is completed, the inadequate Cathedral House at No. 1051 Taylor will be demolished, a Great Stairway entrance, extending up from Taylor St., (as envisioned by the original architect, Lewis Hobart), will allow us a full view of the magnificent, cast-bronze doors (made from the molds of the Renaissance sculptor, Lorenzo Ghiberti).

■ The cornerstone of Grace Cathedral was laid in 1910; the exterior was completed in 1964. The subdued, elegant wrought-ironwork on the gates to the Chapel of Grace, on the south side nearest the California St. entrance, was executed by Samuel Yellin. Murals by Antonio Sotomayor, chronicling cathedral and parish history, are inside the chapel.

■ Acoustics are excellent, and concerts—sacred, secular, organ, choral, or jazz—are regularly presented. Duke Ellington was commissioned by the Diocese to compose a sacred piece, which was performed at a concert in 1965. During the Christmas season of 1990, Bobby McFerrin, the San Francisco singer, organized a 24-hour sing-a-thon "healing", with various musical groups participating.

■ The land on which the Cathedral complex stands was donated to the Diocese by the Crocker family. Charles Crocker was the fourth of the Big Four railroad kings, and the fact that there is now a religious institution on his property is an irony to savor. In retaliation for being denied the adjoining lot to complete his purchase of the square block, Crocker put up a 40-foot-high "spite fence", which cut off the sun and view from Nicholas Yung's house. Crocker's heirs finally bought the property from Yung's estate.

■ We now continue west on California to Leavenworth, to arrive at our beginning.

Walk 4

RUSSIAN HILL SOUTH
Speaking of Intangibles

Every San Francisco neighborhood has its unique ambience—a distillation of the folklore and myths of its early days and the people who lived there. We have only to hear the words, "Nob Hill", and we think resplendent wealth and conspicuous consumption; "Pacific Heights", a more subdued wealth, with mansions, views and spacious lots; "Russian Hill", a craggy, physically compact area with creative people working at their crafts in flats and cottages tucked away among little streets and alleys, yet finding community and inspiration around them.

It's an image, it's an atmosphere, it's an intangible. Russian Hill, traditionally the residence of artists and writers, is no longer affordable to this group. They've moved to other areas, and made their own Russian Hills in Noe Valley, Bernal Heights, and Potrero Hill. Yet Russian Hill retains that elusive, intangible air.

■ We begin at Filbert and Polk, and walk east on Filbert (1300 block). Already we are passing inviting "tuck-ins"—homes barely visible from the sidewalk, like No. 1364, and especially No. 1338 with its wooden stake fence, gardens, and long, brick walk, common to the ten apartment cottages.

■ The 1200 block of Filbert from Larkin to Hyde is composed mostly of Edwardian flats with bay windows on the two upper stories. The block has no trees, but next to No. 1252 is a terraced rock garden. Walking up the narrow, private stairway of No. 1234 must be like walking up the keys of a grand piano. Other charming tuck-ins are on the other side of the street.

■ Continue past Hyde to walk down the Filbert sidewalk stairway. Alto Cottage at No. 1138–1140 has a modified mansard roof, an arbor with a magnolia tree in the center, and numerous bird houses near the wall. A charming Japanese style wooden gate marks the common entrance and garden of Nos. 1112 and 1110, built in 1876.

■ At the bottom of the hill we turn right on Leavenworth. A half-block away, next to 2033 Leavenworth, we ascend Havens Stwy., difficult to find but very charming. At one time, Havens continued through to Hyde; now the only entrance and exit is from Leavenworth.

■ The gardens are cultivated by the property owners alongside the stairway. The fern garden is one of the latest additions to the delightful oasis of green space. In early fall, figs from the beautiful mature tree at No. 14 cover the ground—obviously not the owner's favorite fruit.

Returning to Leavenworth, we turn right (south) toward Union. In the middle of the next block, next to No. 1934 Leavenworth, we turn left on Macondray Lane, one of Russian Hill's secluded pathway/stairways, and follow it to Taylor.

■ The exposed sandstone on the side, the variety of materials employed for the stairway—wood, cobblestones, and brick; and the surrounding

MAP 4

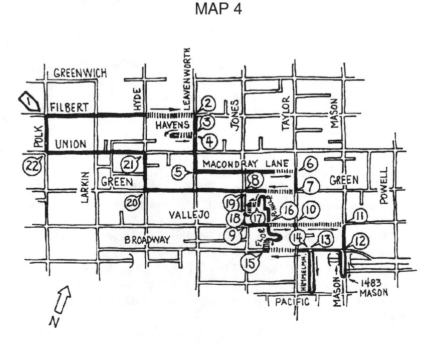

trees and shrubbery in varying shades of green, contribute to the appeal of Macondray Lane, named for a 19th century merchant and viticulturist.

■ Turn right on Taylor, and walk to Green. Ascend the stairway into the cul-de-sac, passing an elaborate Art Moderne apartment house on the left, and an inviting mauve-colored, wood frame house from the 1890s.

■ Towering above everything in sight is No. 999 Green, the Eichler Summit Apartments, built before the height-limitation law was passed in 1970. Three long, open, oval shapes appear in the center of the tower, like huge exclamation points punctuating the end of a special block, the 1000 block of Green that escaped fire and earthquake damage of 1906.

■ Walk to Jones, turn left to walk through the arched, double stairway entrance to a very special section of Vallejo. It is part of Russian Hill's Vallejo St. Crest District, which is on the National Register of Historic Places.

■ One can call this the Livermore section of Vallejo. Since the 1850s, some member of the family has always lived in this enclave and staunchly supported efforts to preserve and maintain the unique character and beauty of the area. One can also call it the Livermore/Willis Polk section because the architect was hired by Horatio Livermore, and later by his son,

---

WALK 4: Russian Hill South Route

Public Transportation: Muni Bus #19 goes on Polk; Hyde St. Cablecar goes on Hyde. Walk two blocks to Polk.

1. Begin at Polk and Filbert. East on Filbert, Descend sidewalk stairway to Leavenworth.
2. Right on Leavenworth.
3. Ascend Havens Stwy., and return to Leavenworth.
4. Right on Leavenworth.
5. Left into Macondray Lane.
6. Right on Taylor to Green.
7. Ascend Green Stwy. to Jones.
8. Left on Jones.
9. Left onto Vallejo Stwy. into cul-de-sac. Walk to end.
10. Descend Vallejo Stwy. next to No. 1019, past Taylor to Mason.
11. Right on Mason. Cross Broadway to see No. 1483 Mason.
12. Cross back to Broadway; left (west) on Broadway.
13. Left to Himmelman Pl.
14. Return to Broadway, continue west on sidewalk stairway past Taylor to Florence.
15. Ascend Florence Stwy.
16. Walk across Vallejo into Russian Hill Pl.
17. Right to walk down ramp to Jones.
18. Right on Jones to Green.
19. Left on Green to Hyde.
20. Right on Hyde to Union.
21. Left on Union to Polk.
22. Right on Polk to Filbert to our beginning.

Norman, to build many of the houses, plus design the entrance on Jones and the stairway to Taylor.

■ We continue to the end of the cul-de-sac, walking on the odd-numbered south side. No. 1045, (originally No. 1023, now No. 40 Florence), was the original Horatio Livermore house, built in 1865. Willis Polk remodeled it, adding a top floor that permitted views in every direction. Three redwood-shingled houses at No. 1030 designed by Joseph Worcester, circa 1889, were demolished by a developer before people realized the treasures they had lost. They have been replaced by the Hermitage condominium apartments which duplicate the Craftsman style, so appropriate for the nooks and crannies of Russian Hill. The style was espoused in the first quarter of the century by Joseph Worcester, Julia Morgan, Bernard Maybeck, Willis Polk and Ernest Coxhead as an antidote to the excesses and formalism of Victorian architecture. The emphasis was on the natural: redwood shingles, protruding eaves instead of bracketed cornices, and gabled roofs. These homes were set into the property to merge with the slope of the land, and the trees and shrubs were an important part of the design.

■ Polk (1867–1924) designed No. 1019 for the artist Doris Williams (we notice the high, half-moon window in her north-facing studio). As part of his fee, the next lot was given to him. Here he built No. 1013 for himself in 1892. The house drops down through six levels, and is now divided into three apartments.

■ In 1915, Laura Ingalls Wilder who wrote the *Little House on the Prairie* series, came to San Francisco to see the Panama-Pacific International Exposition. She stayed with her daughter, Rose, a feature writer for the San Francisco Bulletin, who lived at No. 1019. Laura wrote letters home to her husband in Missouri about the Fair, the City, the people, and life on the hill. These letters have been collected in a small paperback, *West from Home*.

■ The open space at the top of the hill was the 50-vara lot that Horatio Livermore bought in 1889. In 1914, after the residents had subscribed $25,000 for the balustrades and ramps which Polk designed on the Jones side, the top of the summit became the carriage turnaround. Now, the neighbors are reserving it for a planting area.

■ We continue downward on the Polk-designed Vallejo Stwy. Neighbors have banded together to beautify the gardens around the stairway, from the top of the hill to Taylor. Committees have been formed; cleanup days have been well-attended; a landscape architect has been hired; a matching grant from San Francisco Beautiful has helped defray the costs of an irrigation system; the Urban Tree Division of the Dept. of Public Works has arranged for meter installation and water supply; and the community members have taxed themselves in order to maintain the gardens, which will provide delight to everyone.

■ Across from No. 1715 Taylor, we enter the Ina Donna Coolbrith Park, (dedicated in 1911), to walk to Mason. Ina Coolbrith (1841–1928), whose uncle was Joseph Smith, founder of the Mormon Church, came to San Francisco from Illinois, at the age of ten, in the first covered-wagon train that traveled via the Beckwourth Pass in the Sierras. She taught school and later became librarian at the Bohemian Club. Although she was honored as poet laureate of California in 1915, her main contribution to the literary world of San Francisco was as a catalyst to the aspiring writers—Joaquin Miller, George Sterling, Bret Harte, Gelett Burgess and others—who met regularly at her home for readings.

■ Many elderly Chinese people come to the park daily to practice Tai Chi. Their effortless concentration and execution of slow body movements are very much in harmony with the surrounding canopy of Monterey pines.

■ At Mason, we're on the edge of Chinatown and Russian Hill. Turn right for one block, then right again on Broadway. Here we see the dipping and rising of the land, extending to the highest hill south of us, Nob Hill (Walk 3).

■ We are above the Broadway Tunnel, which extends under Russian Hill from Mason to Hyde; it was proposed in 1874, and was opened for vehicular traffic in 1952!

■ We walk across Broadway to No.1483 Mason to see the 69-unit Lady Shaw Center for senior housing which was completed in late 1990. Building above the tunnel was a controversial issue, but the critical need for housing in Chinatown, the fine design by architect Gordon Chong & Associates, and the infusion of private, City, and Federal funding, were decisive factors in favor of construction.

■ Go back across the street, turn left on Broadway to walk in front of the twin-towered Spanish National Church, Nuestra Señora de Guadalupe, at No. 906. The present structure was built in 1912 on the site of the 1875 wooden church. The Archdiocese has closed the church, and it will be used as a Chinese school for several years.

■ Turn left across the street to the mini-park at Himmelman Pl. It is supported by Green Space funds, but its condition alternates between cared for and neglect. Return to Broadway.

■ At the corner of Broadway and Taylor, there is a high retaining wall with decorative edging along the top. Grading of the slopes in the 1860s and 1870s created vertical bluffs. When the streets were lowered, retaining walls and stairways became necessary to protect the houses perched on the top. We walk up the sidewalk stairway on the south side of Broadway

Vallejo Street

for a better view of No. 1020, which is set up high and to the back of the property. This two-story, brown-shingle, Craftsman-style house was designed by Albert Farr in 1909.

■ We ascend the Florence Stwy. next to No. 1032 Broadway, and notice the concrete wall topped with spindle decoration. There's something strange about this stairway. As we approach each landing, the landscape also seems to rise. Nos. 37 and 39 Florence are Pueblo Revival-style with stucco exteriors and deep-set windows to deflect the sun. No. 40, the original Livermore house on Vallejo, has been redesigned by Robert A. Stern.

■ When we reach Vallejo, (Gelett Burgess lived at the corner in the 1890s), we cross the street into Russian Hill Place. Nos. 1, 3, 5, and 7 Russian Hill Place are Willis Polk houses of 1913, built for Norman Livermore. It's hard to believe that Russian Hill possesses such a concentration of bewitching little streets in such a small area!

■ Return to Vallejo, turn right to walk down the ramp to Jones; turn right to Green, and make a left turn. Walk on the south side, the odd-numbered side. The 1000 block of Green was spared from the earthquake and fire of 1906, so it's architecturally notable. No.1011, a brown-shingled house built after the earthquake, was designed around windows previously in the family's possession. No. 1039–43 is an Italianate of the 1880s and was moved here after 1906. No. 1040 was once the home of the Folger family, whose fortune was made from the importing, roasting and packaging of coffee. (San Francisco is also the original home of MJB Coffee and Hills Bros. Coffee.) No. 1055 Green dates from 1866, and was later remodeled by Julia Morgan. The beautiful carriage house at the rear is now used as living quarters. One can also see the 1857 octagon house, the oldest in the City, at No. 1067 Green. A cupola was added in the 1880s. Octagon houses were in vogue for awhile because they were purported to be beneficial to one's health and sexual vigor. (If you wish to have a tour of the interior of an octagon house, check the hours of the Colonial Dames Octagon at 2645 Gough. Telephone: 441-7512.) The 1907 Tudor Revival-style firehouse across the street was formerly occupied by Engine Company No. 31. It is now a National Trust Property.

■ When we reach Hyde, turn right, and then left on Union St. The many neighborhood stores near Hyde and Union make shopping a multistop session. A restaurant now stands where the Marcel and Henri charcuterie served the community for 20 years. The Home Drug at 1200 Union has been in the same family since 1912, and still serves customers who first came to them in the 1930s. The Searchlight Market has been here for sixty years under various owners. A repair shop, the original Swensen's ice-cream parlor, an auto service, and more cleaners, are all within reach.

These shopkeepers symbolize the continuity and stability that contribute to the intangible that is Russian Hill.

■ We continue west on Union to Polk, turn right to Filbert, to our beginning.

Walk 5

RUSSIAN HILL NORTH
San Francisco Architectural Signatures

From the vantage point of Pacific Heights, Russian Hill appears to be
shaped like a shoe with a square toe. Coincidentally, many sections of
Russian Hill are accessible only to walkers.

The redwood-shingled, Craftsman-style homes, designed by Northern
California architects Julia Morgan, Willis Polk, and Bernard Maybeck in
the early 1900s, blend well into this terrain. Irregularly-shaped, deep lots
abound, which make some houses—the kind that we call "tuck-ins"—almost invisible from the street. These tuck-ins are as much a part of the
City's architectural signature as the loftier towers also to be seen on this
walk.

■ Our starting point is the northeast corner of Polk St. and Greenwich,
where the hill begins its sharp rise toward Larkin Street. We walk north
on Polk and pass by the four-story Greenwich Court condominium which
takes up 3/4 of the block. Built of cinder block and redwood, this 1989
structure is painted in a pleasing mid-grey color with white window trim,
giving the street added lightness. The apartment house next to it is an
elaborate Spanish-style building in white stucco.
■ When we turn right on Lombard we see the No. 1299 address of the
apartment house, the ceramic-tiled step risers, decorative metal on the
doors and bas-relief on the pillars. The 1200 block on Lombard beautifully
illustrates the congeniality between the interspersed Italianates and
Craftsman-style homes, and between the homes and their location along
the slope of the hill. Nos. 1275 and 1259 are large Italianates; 1267–1263
are redwood-shingled, refurbished Victorians of 1877. The earliest record

MAP 5

WALK 5: Russian Hill North Route

Public Transportation: Muni Bus #19 runs on Polk; #42, #47, #49 run on Van Ness. Walk one block to Polk.

1. Begin at Polk and Greenwich.
2. Walk north on Polk.
3. Right on Lombard. Cross Lombard at No. 1249.
4. Descend Culebra Ter. Stwy.
5. Right up Chestnut Stwy. to Larkin.
6. Right on Larkin. Continue on Larkin to Lombard.
7. Ascend stairway to George Sterling Park. Bear left on path to Greenwich Stwy.
8. Walk on stairway to Hyde.
9. Left on Hyde to Lombard to Chestnut.
10. Detour to 1000 block Chestnut. Return to Hyde and go left.
11. Right on Francisco. Bear right to Chestnut.
12. Across from No. 960 walk up stairway to Montclair to Lombard.
13. Detour right to No. 2319 Hyde. Return to Lombard to Larkin.
14. Left on Larkin to Greenwich.
15. Right on Greenwich to Polk to our beginning.

of water hookup for No. 1257 is May 1878. No. 1249, a San Francisco Stick Italianate is a beautiful flat front tuck-in with a staircase. Built on a hill, it is doubly imposing with its false front.

■ Cross Lombard at No. 1249 to walk down the Culebra Ter. Stwy. The hard-to-see sign is on the side of No. 1246. This is a stairway with 29 steps, three landings, and a coda of two steps.

■ Culebra is a charming alley of flats and single dwellings enhanced by trees, shrubbery, and flowers. No. 60 has a terrazzo stairway and decorative small tiles; No. 50, an eye-catching, curved, five-windowed second story. Nos. 35 and 25 are simple cottages. No. 23 was built in 1911.

■ We come out of Culebra onto the Chestnut Street cul-de-sac. On our right at the corner is No. 1141 Chestnut, a four-storied series of angled sections to maximize the sun and the views for the residents. Walk up the wide stairway shadowed by Monterey pines, with gardens on either side.

■ Forty-eight steps bring us to a landing where a U-shaped, double stairway begins. We walk up the right-hand one, another 64 steps to Larkin Street. Looking back, we see down the Greenwich corridor to the northwest side of San Francisco; from the top of the stairs we distinguish the two dominant forms of that part of the City—the unmistakable dome of the Palace of Fine Arts (Walk 8) and the towers of the Golden Gate Bridge.

■ We turn right on Larkin. A house on the corner has a brass plaque: "2677 Larkin at Chestnut Street." We wish the architect's name and the date were cited.

■ Continue for one block to Lombard; at the southeast corner, we walk up the stairway into the George Sterling Park, named for the poet living on Russian Hill during the 1920s. Seeing the low-lying trunks of the *Leptospermum* trees and the nodules of the exposed roots as we walk along the path gives us a feeling of entering an ancient woods. A bench has been thoughtfully placed to allow us a meditative view of the Marin hills toward the northwest.

■ We bear left on the path past the bench (to the sound of tennis balls against tennis racquets above us) to the Greenwich Stwy. Ascend the very easy 27 steps past the upper landing where there are benches and a mosaic tile wall. Continue another, hardly noticeable 27 steps up onto the sidewalk, and the tennis players and basketball players gradually come into view on our left.

■ The Alice Marble Tennis Courts, also part of the 2.6-acre park, are on Water Department land, the Lombard reservoir beneath supplying 6–8 surrounding blocks. Alice Marble (1913–1990) was born in the small California town of Dutch Flat, and spent some of her growing years in San Francisco. She joined the Golden Gate Park Tennis Club, the training ground for many outstanding players, and from 1936–1940, she was a four-time winner of the National Women's Singles Tennis championship.

■ Walk down 26 steps to Hyde, turn left facing Alcatraz, another San Francisco signature, and continue to Lombard. No. 2222 is a steel-frame, reinforced-concrete, white, eight-story cooperative (1920), one of five built by T. Paterson Ross in the Russian Hill neighborhood. His buildings are rich in interior detail and utilize the latest technology of that era. Ross designed about 200 buildings during a 32-year period. His professional career ended at 49 when he sustained brain injuries from a load of falling bricks while inspecting the Union League Club from an open freight elevator. He died at the age of 84.

■ The intersection of Hyde and Lombard is a splendid place to stop and see the Hyde Street cable car lurching along with its standing-room-only crowd of passengers. Accorded the conductor's full approval, they alight en masse with their cameras pointed toward Alcatraz, the Bay Bridge or Treasure Island. At the clang of the cable car bell, they rush aboard once more to coast down to the next landing on their way to Aquatic Park. We continue walking north on Hyde.

■ Continue to Chestnut. An inappropriately-placed highrise on the corner still suffers that friendless look.

■ On the northeast corner of Chestnut and Hyde was a landmark 12-room house built in 1852 by William Clark, who built the first wharf near the foot of Broadway (Walk 1).

■ I would suggest a detour to the left on Chestnut to experience the ambience of the 1000 block. Between No. 1000 and No. 1080 is a delightful series of three-story mansard roof homes in white and off-white colors. The south side of the street is the back entrance of the Lombardia condominiums, which won the best medium-high density residential award of 1989, given by the Pacific Coast Builders Association. Designed by Hood/Miller, architects, on a lot that was vacant for 28 years, it consists of 10 large town houses and 32 condos. By thoughtful use of scale, space, light and plant materials they created an inviting Mediterranean setting. No. 1089 Chestnut, completed in 1990, has 17-foot ceilings in the living room, and 5,600 square feet of space.

■ Return to Hyde, turn left (north), walk on the right hand side of the street past the Norwegian Seaman's Church at 2454 Hyde. (The Norwegian Government Seamen's Service at 2501 Vallejo Street, is another indication of the number of Norwegian sailors who make port here.) No. 2434 is a five-sided, Bay Italianate. On the left side of Hyde below the sidewalk is the roof of another reservoir. Straight ahead to the north, is the Hyde Street Pier with its famous collection of historic ships. At the end of the block, walk down three steps and turn right onto Francisco St.

Chestnut Street

The Francisco cul-de-sac is one of my favorites. The large homes here, in a variety of styles and set on several levels of land, command enviable views from either side of the street.

The frame two-story at No. 825 is originally dated 1849, but has undergone many renovations. It was constructed of timber salvaged from ships abandoned in the Bay during the Gold Rush. No. 828 Francisco, at the end of the cul-de-sac, has a bay of leaded windows with octagonal inserts, a modified mansard roof and beautiful copper chimney stacks that have acquired a greenish cast over the years. A fence espaliered with roses follows the slope of the hill.

We stand on the parapet next to No. 800 Francisco to gaze at the variety of architectural shapes and signatures that are part of a San Franciscan's daily eyeful: the abundant, sword-shaped leaves of a palm tree at the lower corner of the street, the square Romanesque tower of the San Francisco Art Institute, the rectangular towers of the Bay Bridge, the conical towers of Saints Peter and Paul Church in North Beach, the cylindrical Coit Tower, and the pyramidical Transamerica building.

Walk along the retaining wall, bearing right (south) to Chestnut.

Turn right on Chestnut. No. 930 is a flat roof. No. 944, built in 1864, has columns and a balcony. Across the street from No. 960 we walk up 28 steps to Montclair Ter., a hidden court of homes and gardens. No. 66, designed in 1956 by one of my favorite architects, Henry Hill, has simplicity and flourish. Next to No. 4, we are at Lombard Street, where drivers enjoy the unusual ride down the most photographed, photogenic hairpin-turn street in the country. (Eight turns within an 800-foot-long section with a grade of 18.18%.) It was designed by City engineer Preston Wallace King in 1922, from a 26% grade, cobblestoned Lombard.

We turn right to walk up a straight, comfortable stairway, and at the top, detour right on Hyde to see No. 2319, a Willis Polk house designed for Robert Louis Stevenson's widow, Fanny, who lived there from 1899–1908. (Lombard and Hyde was purported to be Stevenson's favorite San Francisco corner.) Return to Lombard and walk right to Larkin; turn left. Among the apartment houses is a two-flat Victorian, No. 2545–2543. No. 2531 is a Stick-style Italianate with a picket fence. No. 2515 has rectangular bays, and a fish scale pediment above the windows.

Turn right on Greenwich, to walk down a grooved sidewalk. No. 1342–44 is a new condominium in pleasing pastel colors. The garage has been embellished with a band of decorative ceramic tile placed above doors. Our high spirits continue as we stride by No. 1356, an interesting angular design of concrete landings and steps surrounded by large leafy trees, and arrive at our beginning.

WALK 6

FORT MASON
Pivoting Rakishly Around the Ellipse

On this walk we explore some of the extensive municipal and Federal recreational areas of San Francisco along the northern waterfront. The atmosphere here is highly energized, and the history more apparent than in other neighborhoods.

As we progress from the Marina Green to the Hyde Street Pier, we can appreciate how this land became a focus for Federal military installations, and then slowly evolved under the aegis of the Department of the Interior into land for a national park. The area we traverse is part of the Golden Gate National Recreation Area (GGNRA), the most popular urban park in the United States.

Beginning at the Marina Green, the area is one big, beautiful platform, from which we can pivot out in almost any direction—east to North Beach and Telegraph Hill, southeast toward Downtown, southwest toward Pacific Heights, west to the Palace of Fine Arts, or along the waterfront as we walk today.

The sun's rays, intensified by reflections from the Bay, bestow warmth and good cheer on everything and everybody. People are flying elaborate kites on the Green, people are picnicking, people are jogging and exercising on the parcourse; sounds are coming from every source—the chipping hummingbirds, the calling white-crowned sparrows, the crying gulls, the barking dogs; people laughing and an occasional street vendor sending up a sales holler. The backdrop to all the sights and sounds is the Bay. This is a celebration walk. Here, when there's sun and color and kites and games and laughter, we have to say, "Happy day, everyone!"

MAP 6

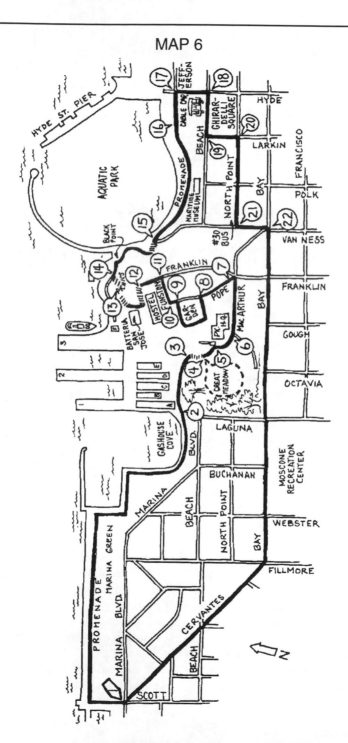

The Fort Mason walk gives me the feeling of dancing my way around a tiered cake. I discover by carefully checking my landmarks, that I am indeed changing elevation, sometimes ever so slightly. Then I realize I can't say for sure what tier I am on, so I have decided to avoid confusion and allow everyone to make an individual count of tiers. I can imagine Fred Astaire savoring this walk. Enjoy

Advisory: The most propitious time to go on the Fort Mason walk is in the morning—a sunny, windless weekend morning.

In addition to being tiered, this walk is elliptical, which means additional walking from the finish to the beginning. To maximize your options at the end of the walk, I suggest coming to the starting point by public transportation. However, if you arrive by car, drive into the Fort Mason driveway, and turn left into the parking lot that faces Marina Blvd. Walk to the beginning.

(Changes to the terrain may necessitate using the walk instructions as suggestions only.)

WALK 6: Fort Mason Route

Public Transportation: Muni Bus #30 goes on Divisadero. Walk two blocks. #30x goes on Beach. Walk two blocks.

1. Begin at Scott and Marina. Follow path along the water, curving around E. Harbor Breakwater. Continue on Gashouse Cove Marina path.
2. Enter the waterfront level of Ft. Mason by the side of Bldg A.
3. Walk up the stairway opposite Bldg.E.
4. Walk on any of the paths around or through the Great Meadow.
5. Pass Bufano sculpture, "Peace ". Pass Phillip Burton Memorial.
6. Left on MacArthur to Headquarter Bldg.
7. Left on Pope.
8. Walk around Community Gardens and out on Pope.
9. Left on Pope.
10. Right on Funston.
11. Left on Franklin.
12. Curve to left on stairway to Bateria San Jose.
13. Descend stairway to Battery. Walk on sidewalk to picnic area; descend stairway to Black Point.
14. Right on footpath; descend stairway to Promenade.
15. Right along Promenade.
16. Continue on Jefferson to Hyde.
17. Right on Hyde to Beach.
18. Right on Beach to Larkin. Walk through Ghirardelli Square.
19. Left on Larkin to North Point.
20. Right on North Point to Van Ness. Check bus schedules for #30, #32 #47–49.
21. Left on Van Ness to Bay.
22. Right on Bay to our beginning.

■ We begin at Scott St. and Marina Blvd., the site of the 1915 Panama-Pacific International Exposition. This extravagant and most classic of all fairs signaled to all the world that San Francisco, like the mythical Phoenix, had arisen from the ashes of the 1906 earthquake to become again the City that everybody loved.

■ Ironically, the underlying foundation of the Marina's existence—water—plus the unstable fill, plus the construction of non-earthquake code buildings, caused catastrophic damage to the neighborhood during the November 17, 1989 earthquake (7.1 on the Richter scale). Residents left the area to find housing in other parts of the City, and some Chestnut St. businesses closed permanently. (Other neighborhoods where streams or lakes had existed also sustained damage).

■ Follow the path along the water, in the direction of Pierce St. (east) curving around the East Harbor Breakwater. (If I were a boat I would protest a name like Winky-Dinky or Lots of Lox). Alongside in the water are coots, western grebes and mallards. Mallow, oxalis and tower of jewels are blooming beside the walkway.

■ We continue on the Gashouse Cove Marina path and enter Fort Mason by the side of Bldg. A. (One can pick up the calendar of events and obtain information here at the Fort Mason Foundation office, or call (415)441-5706.) This level was the point of embarkation for men and supplies since the turn of the century. The buildings alongside the piers were used by the Army through demobilization after World War II, and are now used for recreational and cultural activities. Over 50 nonprofit community and cultural organizations are headquartered at Fort Mason in exchange for reasonable rent. Theaters, museums, music schools, dance classes, computer groups, Children's Art Center, Lawyers for the Arts, and Media Alliance are some of the groups. Greens in Bldg. A is an excellent vegetarian restaurant operated by the Tassajara Zen Center.

■ In Fort Mason, an area of about 300 acres, we can trace a continuous evolving historical line from 1797 to the present, from Spanish and American military fortifications to a new urban national park. Integrating history and land-use objectives is resulting in a unification of the past and present. For instance, as military artifacts from the past are unearthed, they are placed for viewing in contextual areas, necessitating the redesign of spaces and trails. More recent history is also being commemorated: the Phillip Burton Memorial is re-landscaped to accommodate viewing of the sculpture, the green spaces and new paths.

■ Problems areas are continually monitored by the Park Service. They plant native soil-huggers like sand verbena, ice plant and dune daisy to restrain the constantly shifting, sandy soil. They build stairways to prevent erosion, to preserve the fragile topsoil and to keep people on the trails.

■ We pass Bldgs. A, B, C and D, and Piers 1 and 2. The World War II Liberty Ship, the Jeremiah O'Brien, built in a record 56 days in 1943, is permanently stationed at Pier 3. For a nominal charge, one can go on the ship to inspect it during the hours, 11:00A.M.to 4:00P.M.

■ Bldg. F is available for various workshops. On the wall, a mural entitled "Positively Fourth Street" depicts a surreal San Francisco scene that includes a freeway occupied by animals and driverless automobiles.

■ As we continue our walk along the wall, we notice the stern of The Galilee, a Tahitian trading vessel, built in 1891 and in use until 1920. The Oceanic Society has its offices nearby.

■ Opposite Bldg. E is a stairway where, as we walk up the first series of steps, we see hummingbirds dipping and revolving around one another in their courtship ritual. A Monterey cypress is on our left.

■ Continuing upward to the next level, we turn around and see the Marina Blvd., Golden Gate Bridge and the Marin Headlands. A sign here states, "Shortcuts cause erosion". We take the path to our left, walk around to the Great Meadow on our right, retracing the long-forgotten footsteps of hundreds of men, women and children who lived here in tents after losing their homes in the 1906 earthquake. Refugee Camp No. 5 extended beyond the meadow to the site of the present Safeway store to the west.

■ The military played an important role in San Francisco during the 1906 earthquake: the Navy fireboat anchored off Fort Mason was used to pump water from the Bay to the fire engines along Van Ness Avenue; Fort Mason was the headquarters for General Funston, who put San Francisco under martial law to prevent looting; then, under General Greely, Fort Mason became the relief-supply distribution center. When Mayor Schmitz moved his office here, Fort Mason became the center for coordinating civil and military authority.

■ Continuing on the footpath on the right, we come to the Beniamino Bufano statue of granite and mosaic, dedicated to "Peace." I think this is one of his finest works, and an extra dimension of strength comes through when we are able to stand in such close proximity to it. The Society of Friends of Bufano hopes that all his sculptures will one day be part of a sculpture park. Bufano (1898–1970) was a favorite San Francisco person-ality. He was supported by various benefactors, such as the Powell St. restaurant (now defunct) for which he designed and executed a mosaic mural in return for a lifetime of meals.

■ Walk along the path to the Phillip Burton Memorial, designed by landscape architect Tito Patri; the project sculptor was Wendy Ross. The statue is 10 feet high, but Burton is represented in his everyday, human look—rumpled trousers, emphatic gesture, a scribbled note in his jacket pocket. In 1983, Congress dedicated the GGNRA to Congressman Burton, who was responsible for the Federal legislation that made the GGNRA a reality. The sculpture was unveiled in Spring 1991.

We continue on the path to Park Headquarters, Bldg. No. 201 on MacArthur Street, immediately south of the Community Gardens. One can get information here about the National Parks and directions to the various parts of the GGNRA, (415)556-0560. No. 201 was built in 1901 as a military hospital. After the 1906 earthquake, it was used as an emergency center and a lying-in hospital. According to legend, eight babies were born at Fort Mason the night after the quake.

In the years following 1906, Bldg.No. 201 was used as administrative headquarters for Fort Mason. Among the officers who served here during World War II was a second lieutenant in charge of tracking down missing shipments—his name, Ronald Reagan.

We make a left turn on Pope to walk in front of Headquarters. The tile-roof military housing to our right dates from World War II. Near the corner is the Chapel (1942) and the starting place of the Conversation-Pace Gamefield sponsored by the San Francisco Senior Center. Various exercises are paced slowly enough to allow for conversation.

We walk into the Community Garden to explore. (It is one of 90 community and school gardens in the City.) An active group of gardeners is working and enjoying the camaraderie. Space is available to anyone living in the Fort Mason area, but there is a long waiting list. Return to Pope, and go left.

The San Francisco International Hostel at the end of Pope, formerly a Civil War barracks, is a friendly, clean and inviting place. Some of the guests are lolling about on the grass, others are reading.

From the hostel, we turn right on Funston, and left on Franklin. This part of Fort Mason contains military housing dating from the 1850s. The officers' housing on the east side of Pope St. originated as squatters' homes, put up in the 1850s by prominent San Franciscans who knew valuable real estate when they saw it. The Army repossessed the squatters' homes, and began building up fortifications in anticipation of the Confederate onslaught.

Strong pro- and anti-slavery feelings in California culminated in the famous Terry-Broderick duel in 1859. Senator David Broderick, shot by the hot-tempered pro-slavery Judge David Terry near Lake Merced, died here at Fort Mason in the home of a friend.

We turn left on Franklin (north) and walk north on an inviting path. We pass the Palmer House erected in 1855. Then we come to an open space on our left, once occupied by John Fremont's home from 1859-1861, now scheduled to become a planted area. We curve around to our left and go up the stairs to see the plaque noting the site of the Bateria San

Fort Mason

Jose, a Spanish seacoast defense battery located here in 1797. It was built to protect the Yerba Buena anchorage, now Aquatic Park.

■ Take the path closest to the intertwined Monterey cypress and laurel trees, past the light standard No. 43 and down the short stairway to walk across the area of the battery placements in the wall. The sign says, 1863 Battery.

■ Walk up the railroad-tie steps to where we can look down on the Jeremiah O'Brien. Continue to our right along a concrete sidewalk toward the picnic section. We are standing on what is known as Black Point Lookout, so called because of the dark vegetation provided by the laurel trees. The picnic area was constructed on battery platforms dating back to the Civil War. There are four tables and benches where we can sit and enjoy food and the sublime view, which today features a procession of boats with multicolored sails of pink and green and blue, backlit against the clearly delineated hills of Marin and East Bay.

■ Theoretically, the Bay was well-defended against hostile fleets and, later, aircraft. At one time or another there were Spanish or American coastal batteries on the Marin Headlands, on Alcatraz and Angel Island, Fort Point, and here at Fort Mason. The best-preserved of these antiquated defenses is Fort Point, the Civil War fort under the arch of the Golden Gate Bridge.

■ In front of light standard No. 42, we descend a stairway and follow a long, paved walkway. There is vegetation along the wall, the fruit trees are in bloom, and there are benches we can sit on. We walk past a gate that leads to a private residence. At that point, bear left to continue down the stairs to the street level. We can go to our left and go onto the pier, or we can walk toward our right. We choose the path to the right.

■ The curved concrete wall of Aquatic Park, formerly known as Black Point Cove, was part of the San Jose Point Military Reservation that became Fort Mason in 1882. Pumping Station No. 2, built to supply water in case of earthquake and fire is on the right side of the street. We cross the extension of Van Ness Ave. to be on the water side. Restrooms are housed in a round white structure with incised wavy lines near the roof line to simulate ocean waves—another example of the Streamline Moderne style of the 1930s. The duplicate of this structure is at Hyde Street and Jefferson. We walk along the Promenade along the water, and walk up the amphitheater steps to watch birds and swimmers.

■ The ship-shaped Maritime Museum to the right, founded in 1950, has permanent exhibits of historic ship models and other artifacts of the sea; has an excellent collection of prints, and arranges special exhibitions. Well-informed rangers are available to answer questions. (The extensive Maritime library is located in Building C of Fort Mason.) A very active senior center also uses part of the 1939 Moderne building, which was built as a WPA project during the Franklin Roosevelt administration.

■ We walk east on Jefferson, pass the Dolphin and Swim Club established in 1877. Members still swim in the Bay. Next to it is the South End Rowing Club.

■ The historic ships are docked at the corner of Hyde St. Pier, and one can take an imaginary trip on the Eureka, a passenger ferry; the Thayer, a sailing schooner that carried lumber, salmon, and codfish; or the Wapama, a steam schooner for cargo and passengers.There is a nominal fee to board the ships to help defray the expense of preserving them. The bookstore has an excellent collection of books about the sea and related subjects. It is difficult to stop browsing. At the corner of Hyde on the right hand side is the pumping station dating from 1948.

■ Turn right on Hyde St. and walk along the side of Victorian Park, which is festive with a gazebo and flowerway and the Cable Car turntable, where jovial crowds of tourists and residents wait to board. Turn right on Beach.

■ Musicians and performers are interspersed among the outdoor stall displays of jewelry, T-shirts, leather belts, pen and ink drawings of San Francisco scenes, and stained-glass mobiles and insets for windows.

■ Continue to Larkin. Ghirardelli Square, at the corner, is a pioneer example of adaptive use of the former chocolate factory (1893). It was converted in 1967 into a well-designed complex of fine-quality specialty shops, and galleries and restaurants. The entrance, via stairways to the plaza, is particularly pleasing. Walk up the stairway to the plaza where people are sitting around a fountain designed by Ruth Asawa. The open spaces, the many areas set aside for meals al fresco, the nearness to the street, and views of the Bay from many sections, create a seductive environment for browsing or buying, or for an enjoyable day in the City that feels like a vacation.

■ Walk out from the plaza in any direction to reach North Point. Continue to Van Ness and turn left (south). We can either board Muni bus #30 to Broderick and Beach (at the Marina Green), or we can walk to our beginning by making a right on Bay to Scott and Marina Blvd. Excellent refreshments and meals are available on Chestnut, the authentic shopping street of the Marina, between Fillmore and Divisadero.

Walk 7

PACIFIC HEIGHTS
Walk Forward but Always Look Back

When the first cable car went over Nob Hill in 1878, the development of Pacific Heights, the ridge across the Polk-Van Ness Valley, followed soon after. Then as now, the views of the Bay were extraordinary. Although a precipitous 370 feet above sea level, the Heights had many wide, flat lots for the large homes only the wealthy could afford.

The variety of architectural styles ranges from elaborate Queen Anne Victorians of the 1890s, Mission Revival, Edwardian, to mock Chateau. Pacific Heights is an excellent area to practice sightings of architectural details—general, singular, and humorous.

■ We begin at Broadway and Baker St. No. 2898 Broadway, on the northeast corner, was built in 1889 by Bliss and Faville, famous for their designs of classical government buildings. (A few blocks away on Broadway, toward the end of this walk, we will see another Bliss and Faville structure to compare.)

■ Walk north, down the two-block-long Baker Stwy. Monterey cypresses in the center area and dense shrubs on both sides confine the stairway; and the tread-to-riser proportion makes these steps seem steeper than they really are.

■ Entering Vallejo St. from the stairs, we walk into a cul-de-sac with handsome river stones embedded on the slope. The large home to our left at No. 2901 Vallejo, built in 1886, is a combination of Mediterranean and Mission styles. We turn to the right to look at No. 2881 which has an extremely narrow second-story window.

■ Return to Baker to continue walking down the lower section of the stairway, which seems lighter and more cheerful. Open space around the comfortable stairs makes this a happy, bouncy descent. No. 2511 is a redwood-shingled box with a twin-gabled roof.

■ The Palace of Fine Arts is in the center of our view, surrounded by the North Bay and the circle of hills beyond that. To our left on Green are twin houses at Nos. 2800 and 2828 that I find particularly appealing. In fact, let's go to the end of the Green St. cul-de-sac to look at the variety and the unity of architecture.

■ Come back to the corner of Baker and continue walking on Green to Fillmore. No. 2790 is the Russian Consulate. No. 2423, built in 1891, has a ramp to the house; No. 2452 is a tuck-in; No. 2411 has a slate roof. Between Pierce and Steiner, the street is barricaded during the lunch hour so the students from St. Vincent de Paul School can play in the street.

■ The odd-numbered houses in the 2200 block between Steiner and Fillmore have high retaining walls—a reminder of the height of the hill, originally. (If you would like to see the Sherman House, one of the most exquisite B&Bs, walk one block farther to No. 2160, an elegant Bed & Breakfast that has Landmark status. It was built in 1867 for Leander Sherman of Sherman Clay music stores. It was designed especially for musical gatherings, and artists such as Madame Schumann-Heink and Ignace Jan Paderewski performed there. In the back is a rather elaborate carriage house with mansard roof and shingles in alternating patterns of diamonds and octagons. Some of the walk lights in front of the carriage house show the purple tint of oxidation.)

■ Ascend the Fillmore sidewalk Stwy. from Green to Vallejo. It's interesting to note the difference between the styles of the stairway on the left, a complete tread, and the one on the right, a sloping tread. No. 2323 Vallejo is the Vedanta Society Temple designed by Henry Gutterson and completed in 1959. (It is much more subdued than the 1905 original temple (still used) on Filbert and Webster.) The basic philosophic tenet of Vedantism is that all paths to God are equally true. Everything comes from the divine spirit, and the purpose of life is to discover that spirit as it unfolds within us and everywhere else. The monastery and convent are nearby, where men and women train to become monastics.

■ Turn left on Vallejo for one block. The graceless apartment structure at #2295 is a vivid contrast to #2255, four charming brick and stucco set-back apartments built on two levels and sharing a common stairway and landscaped courtyard. At Webster, we walk up the stairway to Broadway. This is one of San Francisco's most famous views. Two estates close by, once belonging to the Flood family, are now private schools: No. 2120 Broadway, built in 1898 for James C. Flood, one of the Comstock bonanza kings, is the Sarah Dix Hamlin School for Girls. The gardens and tennis courts extend down the depth of the lot to No. 2129 Vallejo, where an addition to the school was built in 1965; the two buildings are connected by a stairway. No. 2222 Broadway, the Convent of the Sacred Heart High School, was designed in 1912 for James L. Flood, J.C.'s son. This Italian Renaissance-style mansion by Bliss and Faville has an exterior of Tennessee marble; the interior has hand-carved wood paneling of oak and satinwood and walnut. (I'm reminded that the Hebrew tradition of placing honey on the first page of the first book a child reads, to promote sweet associations with learning, must apply to learning that takes place in beautiful surroundings.)

■ No. 2550 Webster, a heavy-looking, uninviting, clinker-brick structure, was built by Willis Polk in 1896 for William Bourn, who at various times was the head of the Spring Valley Water Company, Pacific Gas and Electric, and the Empire Mining Company in Grass Valley. (Polk also designed Filoli, Bourn's garden estate in Woodside, now part of the National Trust for Historic Preservation.) No. 2550 sports a pineapple finial, architectural symbol of hospitality

■ The Newcomer High School at Jackson and Webster provides bilingual classes and transitional education for recently-arrived immigrant students.

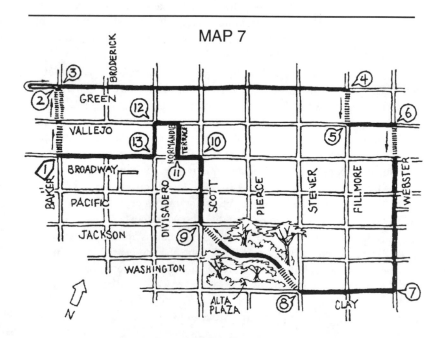

MAP 7

■ Between Jackson and Washington are a series of slanted-bay Italianates, Nos. 2321–2315, that date from about 1875. Their charm is perfectly complemented by the hollyhocks and roses growing in the gardens. In the next block, between Washington and Clay is a series of attached, slanted-bay Italianates, Nos. 2253–2239. Across the street from another group of Italianates, (Nos. 2221–2209), is the Smith-Kettlewell eye research clinic. The California Pacific Medical Center that presently dominates the area has evolved from previous medical facilities. Right turn on Clay.

■ At Steiner, walk up the Clay Stwy. of Alta Plaza Park, 11.89 acres that were purchased in 1877. The stairways are magnificent and the views varied. The series of Italianates on Clay (Nos. 2637–2673), some flat-front, some five-sided, circa 1875, are delightful to view from the hill.

■ We walk across in a westerly direction toward Jackson and Scott; continue north on Scott until Broadway. Left turn to Normandie Ter., a special enclave of a few custom-designed homes. From the cul-de-sac turn left on Vallejo to Divisadero, and again left to Broadway. The view from here is another "special"

■ Turn right on Broadway to Baker to our beginning

WALK 7: Pacific Heights Route

Public Transportation: Muni #3 goes to Jackson and Baker; #45 goes to Union and Baker.

1. Begin at Baker and Broadway. Descend Baker Stwy. to Vallejo; sidewalk stairway down to Green.
2. Left on Green cul-de-sac to see Homes.
3. Continue east on Green to Fillmore.
4. Right to ascend stairway to Vallejo.
5. Left on Vallejo.
6. Right on Webster Stwy. Continue to Clay.
7. Right on Clay to Steiner.
8. Walk up the Clay Stwy. of Alta Plaza Park. Walk across in a westerly direction to Jackson and Scott.
9. Right on Scott to Broadway.
10. Left on Broadway for 1/2 block to Normandie Ter.
11. Go to end of cul-de-sac. Left on Vallejo to Divisadero.
12. Left on Divisadero to Broadway.
13. Right on Broadway to Baker to our beginning.

Walk 8

PRESIDIO WALL & MARINA
Tripping Lightly

Marina neighborhood is one of the most beautiful in the City. The harbor, the boulevard, the Palace of Fine Arts and its surrounding lagoon and paths, and the proximity to the Presidio are magnets for bringing people from everywhere out to enjoy a Day in the City.

The Marina has come full circle: it occupies the landfill site of the spectacular Panama-Pacific International Exposition of 1915, which celebrated the rebirth of San Francisco after the 1906 earthquake. In 1989, because it is built on landfill, the Marina was devastated in the Loma Prieta earthquake. (A miniature replica of the Exposition's magnificent buildings, including the Tower of Jewels and the Fountain of Energy, may be seen at the Presidio Army Museum in the Presidio.)

One apartment building burned, others crumbled, many residences were declared unsafe, and occupants of the area had to leave. (Other areas of the City that were built over a creek or stream, such as parts of the Sunset and the Richmond, also suffered much damage.)

Almost two years later, most of the Marina had been rebuilt. This time, all structures were built or retrofitted to earthquake code. Chestnut St., the Marina's delightful, authentic and stable shopping area (many storekeepers along the street have been in business for over 35 years) is again thriving.

■ We begin at Pacific and Lyon Sts., walking along the edge of the Presidio wall, and enjoying a splendid view of the Palace of Fine Arts, with its stunning, columned, Romanesque rotunda, and with the Marin hills serving as a backdrop.

■ At Broadway, we descend the imposing Lyon St. Stwy. It was designed by Louis Upton in 1916, and is an arrangement of stairs and landings and garden spaces. The Broadway neighbor on the right of the stairway has taken the initiative to have the gardens renewed. The slope is covered with ivy and, much to my surprise, it has a beautiful undulating effect as one walks on the stairs. Plum trees are planted, and annuals along the borders express colors and shapes that draw unsuspecting walkers up the stairs. The 130 steps come to a rest on Vallejo before resuming with another 124 across the street.

■ Five and a half blocks along, cross Richardson at Francisco St. and continue on Lyon to the Palace of Fine Arts. The area around the lagoon is a popular place for people to picnic and to sun, and for wedding parties to be photographed. It's an irresistibly romantic location.

■ We bear left around the theater to the Exploratorium, a museum where adults and children may participate actively—touching, seeing, listening, moving—in experiments that illustrate the scientific principles of perception. The Exploratorium was the brainchild of the late physicist, Dr. Frank Oppenheimer and his wife, Jackie. High-school students serve as docents, explaining exhibits upon request. The Exploratorium is one of the most vital museums in the City, and has been a model for science museums throughout the world.

■ At the Exploratorium's Baker St. exit, we turn into the path that fronts some Baker St. homes, and circles the lagoon, among the Monterey cypresses. We sight a European widgeon, a bufflehead, and some coots. The area on the south side of the lagoon is known as Walter S. Johnson Park. A plaque on a fluted planter records that Johnson, a millionaire who lived across the street, helped preserve this Bernard Maybeck building, the only architectural survivor of the 1915 Fair's many temporary structures.

■ The Spanish-style architecture that is typical of the Marina seems to reflect all the sunlight. We turn left (east) on Bay. A mural of an English touring car and chauffeur is on the garage next to No. 2380. A tile inset of a Spanish lady with a mantilla is on the wall of No. 2375. There are flats and single dwellings along the block. No. 2300 is a 15-unit apartment building. The original building was damaged by the 1989 earthquake, and the present structure is new.(The owner carried earthquake insurance.)

■ We see several apartment buildings that have undergone extensive renovation and now have FOR RENT signs. We are told that the prices are equal to other neighborhoods, that people are rapidly returning to the

MAP 8

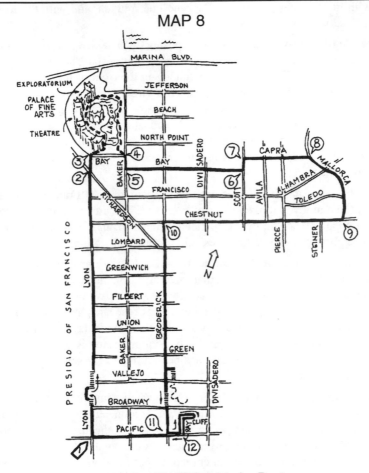

WALK 8: Presidio Wall & Marina Route

Public Transportation: Muni #3 or #43 stop one block away from start.

1. Begin at Lyon and Pacific. Walk north on Lyon to Richardson and Francisco.
2. Cross Richardson to the Exploratorium.
3. Bear left to walk on Palace Dr. around the back of theater & Exploratorium. Continue around inner courtyard of rotunda and walk among the ruins. At Baker St. entrance of Exploratorium, right on path that circles lagoon.
4. Walk south on Baker to Bay.
5. Left on Bay to Scott.
6. Left on Scott to Capra.
7. Right on Capra to Mallorca.
8. Right on Mallorca to Chestnut.
9. Right on Chestnut to Broderick.
10. Left on Broderick to Pacific.
11. Left on Pacific to Raycliff.
12. Return to Pacific. Right to Lyon to our beginning

Marina because they have enjoyed living here, and because they have a belief that disaster will not strike twice.

■ Turn left on Scott and right on Capra. At the corner of Avila is a beautiful row of two-story dwellings. No. 144–146 is a Spanish-style with wooden shutters. No. 196 Avila is a two-story tunnel bungalow with a beautiful garden and abundant greenery along the sidewalk. Two apartment buildings at the corner of Pierce were damaged by the 1989 quake.

■ We turn right on Mallorca to Chestnut; then right on Chestnut, the Marina's shopping street. Lucca Delicatessen at No. 2120 has been here since 1931, and is still operated by the founding family. Their homemade pastas and sauces, barbecued chicken and custom-made sandwiches are favorites for which long lines of customers wait while visiting with one another. Lucca is a neighborhood institution.

■ Ratto's Hardware & Housewares and La Seine Bakery, businesses that had been on the street for over a generation, have been replaced by other businesses. Peets, at No. 2156, retains the name of Alfred Peet, the person responsible for educating the Bay Area about fine coffees and teas, although he no longer owns it. Fortunately, two experienced coffee people bought it, and continue the tradition of Peet's roasting.

■ San Francisco Federal has old kerosene fixtures on the exterior. The Chestnut Street Grill is in a building that has traditionally been a bar/restaurant since the '30s. Jack's Newspapers and Magazines at No. 2260 has publications from all major cities.

■ No. 2323 has been a grocery store for approximately 50 years; it is Marina Super since 1960. They have charge accounts and make home deliveries. Mathray's Flowers at No. 2395 and Frank's Shoe Repair at No. 2412 have been on the street since the 1950s. (Frank's has a shoe deposit box in the door.) The apartments at No. 2442 and No. 2465 date from 1930 and 1928.

■ Turn left on Broderick to walk uphill. The houses are eclectic and architecturally sound. No. 2821 and the house next door were the earliest houses on the block, dating from about 1907.

■ At Broderick and Vallejo, we come to an overpass stairway that leads into the driveway and garage of No. 2798 Broderick. The landscaping here counteracts the steepness of the hill beautifully: three pine trees planted among large riverbed rocks laid out in a pleasing pattern in the center of the street, with cobblestones outlining the margins. Toward Broadway, Broderick becomes a miniature "curly Lombard Street."

■ Up a stairway of 19 steps plus a sidewalk of 21 steps, we arrive at No. 2800 Broadway, a 1907 Jacobean-style mansion designed by Willis Polk. It features early-Renaissance stone archways and leaded windows; a

Lyon Street

magnolia tree blooms out front. No. 2801 Broadway, with its Corinthian columns, cries out for cascading greenery to clothe the bare walls.

■ From this height, it is hard to believe we recently left the Palace of Fine Arts.

■ We continue on Broderick. At Pacific, we detour left for about 50 feet for a look at Raycliff Ter., a charming cul-de-sac of six houses designed by contemporary architects.

■ We turn around and walk west on Pacific. The El Drisco Hotel, built in 1903, has 50 rooms, and was probably the earliest hotel to be situated in a residential area. It has been under the same ownership since 1944 and continues to carry on their tradition of personal service to their guests.

■ The two empty lots next to No. 2950 belong to the Unified School District. No. 2950 is a "tuck-in" house, placed at a distance from the sidewalk. An unusual variance gives three houses at No. 3070 one driveway with entrances on both Pacific and Lyon St.

■ Turn right to Lyon to our beginning.

Walk 9

LAND'S END
Sutro Land and the GGNRA

This walk goes through the westernmost section of San Francisco, an area closely identified with Adolph Sutro, who arrived in the city in 1850 from Aix-La-Chapelle. He is one of my favorite San Francisco pioneers.

Sutro was trained as an engineer, but worked in the tobacco business until the silver strike in the Comstock mines. Floods and noxious fumes had almost halted operations; Sutro designed a tunnel that would have drained and ventilated the mines, not only saving the lives of miners but increasing output as well. The owners, Ralston, Fair and Flood saw Sutro as a threat to their profits and refused to finance the tunnel project.

Sutro was persistent, obtained financial help from the East, sold his invention, and invested the profits in San Francisco real estate.

An avid horticulturist, Sutro planted trees everywhere. Entomologists and botanists decry his selection of non-native plants because they altered the area's ecology. It's difficult to walk in San Francisco without being aware of his influence. He was responsible for foresting the Presidio, Fort Mason, Mount Sutro, and Yerba Buena Island (the mound of land that anchors the Bay Bridge) with eucalyptus.His Sutro Heights home was a 21-acre estate of sculpture-crowded, landscaped gardens. The house has long been gone, but the garden is open to the public as part of the Golden Gate National Recreation Area.

One of Sutro's best-known contributions to the City was the famous Cliff House; indeed, two of three Cliff Houses. The first two (1863–1894 and 1896–1907) were destroyed by fire. The second and third were built by Sutro, and the surviving third has been modernized since 1950.

MAP 9

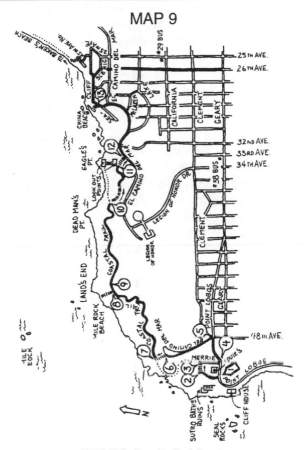

WALK 9: Land's End Route

Public Transportation: Muni #38 stops at 48th Ave. and Pt. Lobos Ave. Walk 2 blocks. Muni #18 stops at Louis' Restaurant.

1. Begin at No. 902 Pt. Lobos Ave. behind Louis' Restaurant and walk down trail to stairway
2. Ascend stairway to Merrie parking lot.
3. Right through lot to Pt. Lobos Ave.
4. Left on Pt. Lobos Ave to El Camino Del Mar.
5. Left on El Camino to Monument.
6. Descend stairway near monument to Coastal Trail.
7. Right on Coastal Trail.
8. Descend stairway at 2nd hiker's marker.
9. Return to Coastal Trail. Continue to left.
10. Ascend stairway to right at sign "No Walking On Coastal Trail."
11. Left to descend stairway to Eagle's Pt. Lookout. Return to El Camino.
12. Left on El Camino to Scacliff to China Beach.
13. Return to 33rd and Geary via Scenic Way to 26th or any one of the Avenues; or continue to 25th Ave. north to Baker Beach and take the #29 at California and 25th to Geary to the #38 to our beginning.

Another popular recreation spot associated with Adolph Sutro was the Sutro Baths: seven indoor salt-water pools, each heated to a different temperature, with room for 10,000 swimmers; seats for 7,000 spectators; palms and Egyptian relics in the plant conservatories—truly a DeMille spectacle.

(Note: We strongly suggest you walk along the designated trail. This is an extra-sweater walk. The temperature can change capriciously. Also, don't forget binoculars.)

■ The walk starts behind No. 902 Point Lobos Ave. (Louis' Restaurant as this is written), on a footpath beside a yellow railing. Below are the ruins of Sutro Baths, opened in 1896, closed in 1952 and destroyed by fire in 1966. Broken columns, fragments of tile mosaic, and the emptied pool area extend toward the ocean. The eroded sandstone setting and the offshore Seal Rocks add to the melancholy drama of the site. The whole seems right for the unfolding of a Greek tragedy.

■ From the path we walk up a capacious eight-foot-wide, railroad-tie stairway to Merrie Way parking lot. This stairway supersedes a sand ladder that was built in 1981 under the direction of James Milestone, a ranger with the Golden Gate National Recreation Area. He had seen a similar ladder on a dune north of Amsterdam and adapted the idea for Land's End. There are sand ladders at Fort Funston and at Tennessee Cove.

■ Plants native to the sand dunes are being encouraged by park botanists. Along the way, we see dune tansy, blue bush lupine, beach primrose, and coyote bush. The area sometimes suffers landslides during heavy winter rains, so parts of the trails may be closed. We just walk on the alternate path indicated when necessary.

■ We make a right turn through the parking lot, and a left on Point Lobos Ave. Turn left on El Camino Del Mar, and continue to the stairway near the monument. Descend to the Coastal Trail, which we follow to the stairway down to the Point Lobos lookout. This stairway is made of recycled railroad ties from the never-completed Belt Line Railroad. The chain rails are from some of the historic ships at the Maritime Museum.

■ We turn right on the Coastal Trail, and descend the stairway at the second Hiker's Marker, and follow it to the lookout at Mile Rock Beach. Descend the stairway for a look at the automated Mile Rock Lighthouse.

■ On a clear day much of the Golden Gate National Recreation Area can be seen across the Gate: from west to east past the Headlands of Marin— Tennessee Cove, Rodeo Beach, Bird Island, the lighthouse at Point Bonita, Bonita Cove, Conzelman Road, Point Diablo, Kirby Beach, and the Golden Gate Bridge. Land's End is the outcropping of rock to our right.

Land's End

We walk back up the stairway and continue to the left to Painted Rock, a Coast Guard marker. (It was used as a sight-line with Point Bonita Lighthouse.) Ascend the stairway to the right at the sign stating "No walking on Coastal Trail."

Left turn down the stairway to Eagle's Point Lookout. Here we have a good view of the beaches; we see Fort Point. Eagle's Point once had 28 trees, but 26 of them died of exposure caused by people trampling on the roots. When the stairway was built in 1980, the Park Service raised the ground level to protect the tree roots, and made sure that the railroad ties fitted over them.

This particular kind of stairway is called a *gabion*, French for a certain type of basket used in agriculture. We can see that the side with a basket-weave pattern is actually a retaining wall, with risers to hold the wall in. The whole system was built up so that people would have a level tread to go across.

We come back up the stairway and take the path to El Camino del Mar and 32nd Ave. Houses, yards and automobiles are in stunning contrast to the sunning seals and earthen footpaths of a moment ago! Land's End Trail ends here, where the old streetcar route began. The Geary bus is two blocks south.

■ We have several alternatives, depending on your mood. From El Camino del Mar, we can go right to the Legion of Honor, then board the #18 bus back to our beginning. There is a lunchroom in the Museum (entrance fee) or we can lunch in the Lincoln Park golf clubhouse.

Otherwise, we continue on El Camino del Mar to Seacliff toward China Beach. A stone has been placed at the top of the China Beach Stwy. to commemorate the Chinese fishermen who used this site. China (formerly James D. Phelan) Beach is well maintained, with lifeguards, a bath house, picnic tables, and benches from which to watch boats. Or to contemplate....

We return to 33rd and Geary via Scenic Way to 25th Ave., or anyone of the avenues, or we can continue to 25th Ave. north to Baker Beach. The #29 bus stop is near Baker Beach; take it to Geary, then hop on the #38 to our starting point.

Country and town, nature and people. This side of the City, along the ocean, once used for military fortifications by the Spanish and the Americans, is now mostly sand dunes, scrub habitat and space. The eastern side of San Francisco that was once Yerba Buena, a perfect site for commerce, fishing and shipping, is now a high-density commercial and residential area.

The map of San Francisco shows large expanses of green north and east from the Cliff House on the Great Highway, all the way to Hyde St.

It's a wonder to have almost 4,000 acres of the City in the Golden Gate National Recreation Area!

■   Now we can go back to our starting point on foot, or by taking the #38 Geary bus from 33rd Ave. and Geary.

Walk 10

GOLDEN GATE HEIGHTS
Lead Thread on a Sugar Sack

The vast tract of land known as the Sunset District sprawls from Sloat Blvd. to Golden Gate Park and from Stanyan St. to the Pacific Ocean. At one time, it was all sand dunes, and a Sunday's outing to the beach,with lunch or dinner at the Cliff House on the Great Highway, was a gala occasion.

Silting is a continual problem, but it has been minimized on the Great Highway by a new design of raised paths for bicyclists and pedestrians, plus the planting of dune tansy and ice-plants.

The outer Sunset gets wind and fog, magnificent sunsets, the ocean view and clear, clean air.

The establishment of Golden Gate Park in 1870 facilitated the settlement of the Sunset. Other events continued the process: a railroad along H St.(Lincoln Way) to the beach in 1879 and the Midwinter Fair in Golden Gate Park in 1894; the establishment of U.C. Medical School in 1898, St. Anne's Church in 1905 and the earthquake of 1906.

Mass housing techniques perfected in the 1920s, were utilized by the three leading contractor/builders in the Sunset—Doelger, Galli and Gellert, who were able to sell homes in the late 1930s for $5,000. Production recommenced after 1945. The development of the homes with the tunnel entrance, or the "Sunset look", solved two problems: the smaller lots, 25' x 65', and the low, maximum $6,000 FHA loans. Sixty to eighty percent of the homes are owner-occupied.

The Sunset has a stable, varied population consisting of middle-class families of many different racial origins, the most recent being Asians.

64

According to the 1990 census, Asians comprise 45%, whites, 47%, blacks, 2% and Latinos, 6% of the Sunset population.

One of the Sunset's many subdivisions is Golden Gate Heights. Scouting out the walk here was reminiscent of trying to open a sugar sack with one movement. I had to find the beginning loop thread that automatically unlocked the other loops, and voila! the sack was open. When I found the lead stairway in the Golden Gate Heights neighborhood, all the other stairways "unlocked" and I felt as if I was on a Matisse walk—just one uninterrupted line with many curves.

■ We begin at Kirkham and 15th Ave., and walk up the stairway next to No. 1501 15th.

■ We take the 160 steps upward at a slow pace to enjoy the view from each landing. At the fourth landing, we can see the twin spires of St. Ignatius Church to the northeast. At the fifth landing, toward the right, St. Anne's of the Sunset Church is in view, and behind it, toward the right, the Byzantine dome of the Temple Emanu-el. Behind us toward the north are the Marin hills and the orange towers of the Golden Gate Bridge, half-hidden by the scalloped tops of the trees in Golden Gate Park. At Lawton and Lomita, we come at last to the top of the stairway.

■ Turn slightly to the right and walk on the odd-numbered side of Lomita for the views between the houses. At the intersection of Lomita and Aloha, bear left on Aloha. At the intersection of Aloha, 15th Ave. and 14th Ave., cross the street and bear left onto 14th, walking on the upper separation.

■ We ascend the stairway into Grand View Park on our right, a superb place to watch the sunset. The park is the habitat for several native plants, bush lupine and beach strawberry and bush monkey flower and coyote bush; the rare and endangered plants here are the Franciscan wallflower and the dune tansy. Grand View Park is being restored under the aegis of the Native Plant Society and the Friends of Open Space.

■ We come to two wooden benches, and walk around to the right for the view. There's a hill of windblown sand here, but underneath is chert, reddish in color, imbedded with pieces of radiolarian. Geologists have found this material at hundreds of feet below sea level, and have dated it at 100,000,000 years.

■ At the point where we can go no farther, we walk on the uphill path, and near a mature Monterey cypress tree, turn to the right. A praiseworthy wooden floating stairway, accented with a wooden handrail, has been built. A very nicely sited, wood-slat bench on the landing allows us to look out over the ocean.

■ We turn to the right to walk down the stairway. In the distance, Golden Gate Park looks like a sea of green as it cuts a swath across the two sections of the city. St. Anne's Church stands out like a sentinel. One can't think of the Sunset neighborhood without thinking St. Anne's. The curving street that snakes through the park is 19th Ave. Another information placard about Grand View Park is strategically placed at the bottom of the stairs so that we see it and read it.

■ We turn to our left, and walk on the upper portion of Noriega. Crossing 14th Ave. (near No. 1762), we can only veer to our left. We are now at the corner of Ortega and 14th, and we turn left on the upper portion of Ortega. The hill on the corner of Ortega and 14th, also being restored by the Native Plant Society, has exposed Franciscan outcropping so expressive of age and power that No. 601 Ortega (1953) which is built up on the rock (and one of my favorite houses), is one of the most dramatic residences in San Francisco.

MAP 10

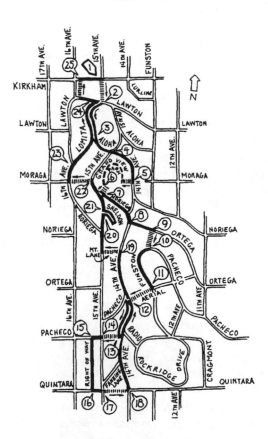

■ The Cascade Stwy. is on the east side of No. 601. We walk up to Pacheco. Carl E. Larsen, a Danish restaurateur, loved this area. By the time of his death in 1924 at age 84, he had given the City six acres of land in the Golden Gate Heights, including Golden Gate Heights Park.

■ At the top of Cascade, we are at Pacheco 900 and Funston 1800. Follow Funston to the right and walk on the odd-numbered side. Across the street from No. 1886 Funston is the Aerial Stwy., which we descend.

■ The bottom of the stairway is at 14th Ave. 1900 and Pacheco 1000. We turn left on 14th Ave. (1900 block). This is a divided street and we're walking on the lower part of it. Somebody planted narcissus and alyssum along the retaining wall. There are also succulents, a Hollywood juniper, and daisies.

WALK 10: Golden Gate Heights Route

Public Transportation: Muni #N Judah Metro stops at 15th and Judah. Walk one block to Kirkham.

1. Begin at Kirkham and 15th Ave. Ascend 15th Ave. Stwy. to Lawton and Lomita.
2. Right turn, slightly. Walk on odd-numbered side of Lomita.
3. Bear left on Aloha at Aloha and Lomita.
4. At intersection of Aloha, 14th and 15th Aves. Bear left on 14th. Walk on upper level.
5. Ascend Grand View Park Stwy. on our right. Walk around to right for view. Walk up hill on path. near cypress tree, turn right onto stairway.
6. Descend to Noriega.
7. Turn left and cross 14th Ave. (No. 1762).
8. Turn left on Upper Ortega at Corner of Ortega and 14th.
9. Right on Cascade Stwy. (east side of No. 601 Ortega). Ascend to Pacheco 900 and Funston 1800.
10. Follow Funston to the right. Walk on odd-numbered side.
11. Descend Aerial Stwy. (next To No. 1895 Funston) to 14th Ave.
12. Left turn on 14th Ave.—lower level—1900 block. At fork of upper and lower 14th Aves., walk on lower.
13. Descend Mandalay Lane Stwy. At the crossroads of Radio 000 and 14th 2000. Stairway ends next to No. 1998 15th.
14. Cross 15th (2000 Block). Walk downhill on Pacheco (1100).
15. Left into right-of-way next to No. 1125 Pacheco.
16. Left on Quintara to 15th.
17. Ascend Quintara Stwy. (next to No. 60 Fanning) to 14th.
18. Left on 14th onto upper level.
19. Descend Mount Ln. Stwy. next to No. 1795 14th to 15th.
20. Right on Sheldon. Make U turn.
21. Right on 15th to No. 1701 15th.
22. Descend stairway to 16th Ave.
23. RIght on Lomita to Lawton.
24. Left on Lawton to descend stairway next to No. 970 Lawton.
25. Right on Kirkham to our beginning.

We come to the crossroads of Radio 000 and 14th Ave. 2000. A few feet farther on is the Mandalay Lane Stwy. Mandalay is inscribed in the sidewalk. We walk down, enjoying the ocean view.

Cross 15th Ave. 2000, and continue down Pacheco 1100. To our right we see Grand View hill, and the new stairway that we ascended earlier. We are walking downhill on Pacheco. The houses on 15th Ave. are noticeably larger.

Next to No. 1125 Pacheco we turn left into an alley entrance, or right-of-way. Turn left on Quintara to 15th Ave., ascend Quintara Stwy. It's a double stairway that telescopes at the landing into a single.

A thought: What are the possibilities of a *trompe l'oeil* painting that descends all the way down the stairs—and down the pot-metal handrails? The land adjoining the stairway would be a delightful sight filled with trees and flowers.

At the top of the stairs we are at the #6 Parnassus bus stop, on 14th near Quintara. Turn left on 14th onto the upper level, where we can see the ocean breakers. As we continue on 14th Ave. 2000 on the upper level, we see ahead of us the wondrous rock formation on the hill, and we pass the stairway we had descended earlier. No. 1930 14th Ave. is exquisitely gardened with bamboo, holly and cypress. A rope handrail and a rock stairway add an extra touch of compatibility.

We are in the 1800 block of 14th Ave, walking past the descending stairway next to No. 1883 14th Ave. This is the other side of the hill facing Ortega; the side view of the outcropping is awe-inspiring. No. 1843 faces directly onto the Franciscan rock formation. (I'm sure an ocean view is visible from the other side of the house.) The rock reminds me of Hawthorne's short story, "The Great Stone Face". A child spent many hours during his life looking at a configuration in a rock. He identified so much with the face, that people began to realize he looked like the face in the stone.

Next to No. 1795 14th we descend Mount Ln. Stwy. Half-way down on our right is a swimming pool that looks as if it belonged to a group of houses. No. 7 is on the gate.

The stairway ends across from No. 1801 15th Ave. (The #66 Quintara bus goes by here.) While walking on 15th near No. 1774, we decide, for fun, to turn right on Sheldon, a quiet cul-de-sac. Here are the apartments that belong to the swimming pool!

We return to 15th and turn right to No. 1707. The land in front of us, scheduled for a future park, has a beautiful view and many eucalyptus trees.

■ Descend the stairway to 16th. Noriega 800 and 15th Ave. 1757 converge; we continue to our right on 15th. Next to No. 1707 Noriega, we descend the Moraga Stwy., which at this time is in deplorable condition.

■ The hillsides need a great deal of work, but the view of Golden Gate Park to the ocean is without peer.

■ Turn right on 16th Ave. to Lomita. At the crossroads of Lomita and Aloha there's a triangular section with a small stairway that can benefit from shrubs and flowers. Follow Lomita to Lawton. The University of California buildings are to our right; and behind them is the Sutro Forest.

■ Turn left on Lawton to descend the stairway (next to No. 970) to Kirkham. Turn right to our beginning.

■ We can continue north to Judah and Irving Sts. for refreshments. The latter is a personal, friendly, older neighborhood shopping center, with many family-owned stores. In addition, along Ninth Ave. from Judah to Lincoln, are rows of specialty shops, restaurants, bookstores, a shoe shop, a garage painted with murals of Swiss scenes, cafe espresso retreats and a natural-food store.

Walk 11

EDGEHILL
The Hideaway Path

This walk fills in the western gap in the central circle of hills. Edgehill neighborhood ranges along the traffic thoroughfares of Dewey Blvd., Taraval and Claremont. The homes are built around a high hill (600 feet) that determines shapes and widths of streets. The background of eucalyptus trees at times becomes the foreground.

■ We begin at Pacheco and Merced, and turn left on Merced, then right on Hernandez. At the corner, No. 65 Merced, is the Church of Perfect Liberty, a religious group founded by Tokuharu Miki who died in 1938. The mission of Perfect Liberty is to bring about world peace through living the Precepts of "Life is Art" and "Man's life is a succession of self-expressions".

■ Turn right on lower Garcia, and walk up the stairs to upper Garcia near No. 71. Continue right on upper Garcia, and at the crossroads with Edgehill, bear left on Edgehill.

■ Turn left at No. 100 Edgehill Way, a half-timbered house with the sign "Folie a Deux". We walk upward, gradually experiencing the high elevation of Edgehill, and the quietness of the forest. No. 111 Edgehill Way, which curves around the corner, belongs to a well-known builder.

■ The Edgehill Improvement Association began in the 1930s as a poker club for owners of 15 homes. The founding members planted cypress seedlings, painted the white line in the middle of the street so that it would be visible in the fog, and gave talks of general interest. Today each Association member is levied an assessment against emergencies for which the City is not responsible.

No. 250 Edgehill, fronted by a superb rock formation, was built in 1927 (houses below the hill already existed by 1927). The owner/builder remembered picnicking on Edgehill when it was open space. It's not difficult to imagine the hill in its original setting as a wondrous place from which to view the sunrise and sunset, the ocean and the Farallone Islands. Even today, surrounded by pines and cypresses and eucalyptus, the houses on top of the hill have a full view of the Farallones.

■ The splendid stairways of stone and brick that lead to individual homes are an aspect of Edgehill I particularly appreciate. No. 200 and No. 400 are admirable examples. We circle around the hill to the top, and then circle down to the corner of No. 100 Edgehill Way, where we turn to our left.

■ If ever one can use the term, *rus in urbe*—the country in the city—it is here in Edgewood. A quietness and a neighborliness (we effortlessly struck up a long conversation with a resident) and a pride in the environment are evident.

■ Our route leads us to the end of the cul-de-sac and through an opening in the cyclone fence. We bear left, then uphill on a well-marked footpath through the forest. We come to the First Church of the Nazarene parking lot, formerly a working rock quarry (the rock at No. 250 came from here). The defaced hill suffered two washouts in years of heavy rains during which, a resident recalls, boulders the size of small automobiles tumbled down.

■ We walk on the path toward our right, finding large clumps of fennel, remains of concrete objects, and close-up views of the chert, equivocally angled.

■ We reach the macadam paved parking lot; the Church, off to the right, is almost hidden in the rock; tree roots imbedded in stone, are exposed on the side of the hill. When we come to the end of the driveway, we are on Ulloa and Waithman.

■ Right turn on Ulloa. The street is graded in a very inventive way: cars are parked on the upper level; houses are sited on a lower level, separated by a curb, and concrete steps—3 or 4. The uniformity of the line, and the additional separation by trees and shrubs and flowers and green lawns (unusual in the 4th year of the drought) bestow a cozy feeling to the block.

■ At Kensington next to No. 35 we make a right turn into Waithman, a parallel alleyway/access road (they intersect throughout the neighborhood) and continue to Granville. The pedestrian skyway that goes across Portola Drive to the Miraloma neighborhood (Walk No. 26) ends here.

■ At Granville turn left, and then right on Ulloa to see the fronts of the houses. At the corner of Ulloa and Allston stands a magnificent magnolia tree.

■ We turn right at Dorchester, and next to No. 138 we turn right again onto this lovely, divided walkway/stairway. Cross the street and continue on the walkway. This section is a series of pedestrian alley "boulevards" with center plantings that intersect with access alleys. The stairways extend from Dorchester to Allston to Granville.

■ Cross Granville Way. In front of No. 194 is a stairway. We cross another twitton and continue. We see the Mt. Davidson cross to our left. No. 367 has a pattern of variegated lengths and widths of redwood shingles, but the sides of the house are stucco.

■ A long uphill walkway leads us to Kensington and Vasquez End. Turn right on Kensington, and near No. 209 turn left on upper Vasquez. Continue on Vasquez, and next to No. 150, descend the Little Pacheco Stwy., a series of steps and landings; the widest steps at the base on Merced, where benches are built into the wall. The Little Pacheco reso-

MAP 11

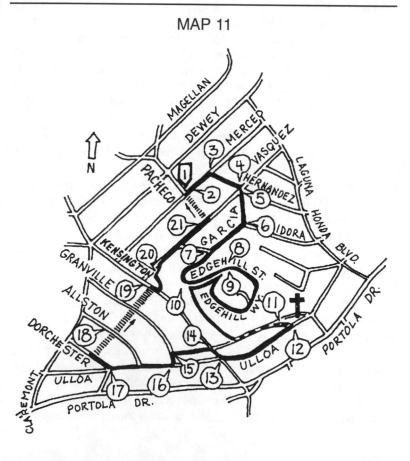

nates with the Grand Pacheco Stwy. across Dewey Blvd. in the Forest Hill neighborhood. The visual effect as we descend is unique in San Francisco stairway walking, and is a testimonial to comprehensive planning. Turn left on Merced to our beginning.

■ The combination of alleys, stairs, planting strips, the woods and soft earth to walk on, makes Edgehill a very special enclave to treasure.

■ For refreshments or a meal, we walk from Claremont Blvd. to West Portal Ave., the authentic neighborhood shopping street. The West Portal Metro station is also there, a convenience if you come by public transportation.

MAP 11: Edgehill Route

Public Transportation: Muni Metro #s K, L, M. Get off at Forest Hill Station.

1. Begin at Merced and Pacheco.
2. Left on Merced.
3. Right on Hernandez.
4. Right on Lower Garcia.
5. Cross Street to Upper Garcia.
6. Right on Garcia.
7. Bear left on Edgehill.
8. Left at No. 100 Edgehill.
9. Circle around top. Return to No. 100 corner of Edgehill.
10. Left on Edgehill.
11. Walk on path. Cross parking lot of Church to Ulloa.
12. Right on Ulloa.
13. At Kensington turn right to alleyway access Rd.
14. Left into alleyway to Granville.
15. Left on Granville to Ulloa.
16. Right on Ulloa to Dorchester.
17. Right on Dorchester to No. 388 to walk on walkway/stwy.
18. Continue past Allston and Granville to Kensington.
19. Right on Kensington.
20. Left to upper Vasquez. Continue to Pacheco Stwy.
21. Left on Pacheco Stwy. down to Merced to our beginning.

Walk 12

FOREST HILL
Marienbad in San Francisco

It's not the longest stairway in the City nor the steepest. Filbert and Vallejo Stwys. are longer; Oakhurst steeper; Vulcan and Harry more charming; Pemberton more personal.

However, the Grand Pacheco Stwy.is by far the most elegant in San Francisco. An urn of flowers 20 feet in diameter introduces this long stairway placed amidst forest and lawns. The stairs themselves—eighteen-and-a-half feet wide, with balustrades, columns and patterns of stones repeating into the distance—lend the setting a dreamlike, rococo quality. We think of Alain Resnais' film, *Last Year at Marienbad*, and easily intermingle the Pacheco Stwy. with the surroundings of Marienbad.

Our rococo walk of curves and curlicues reiterates the innate elegance of this stairway in its Forest Hill setting.

Forest Hill was originally part of the 4,000-acre Rancho San Miguel, granted in 1843 to Jose de Jesus Noe, the last Mexican *alcalde* of San Francisco. After California became independent, the 11 ranchos that comprised the town were subdivided. In 1880, Adolph Sutro bought 1,100 acres of Noe's rancho; Crocker's estate bought the rest.

Public transportation became easily accessible to the western part of the City after the Twin Peaks Tunnel was built. In anticipation of this, the Newell-Murdoch Company began subdividing the Forest Hill tract in 1912, cutting down much of what had been extremely dense forest planted by Adolph Sutro and his troops of eager school children. Difficult engineering and construction problems were solved in a most aesthetic manner by Mark Daniels, the landscape engineer, who deserves a plaque commending his designs of curving streets, generous stairways, ornamental

74

MAP 12

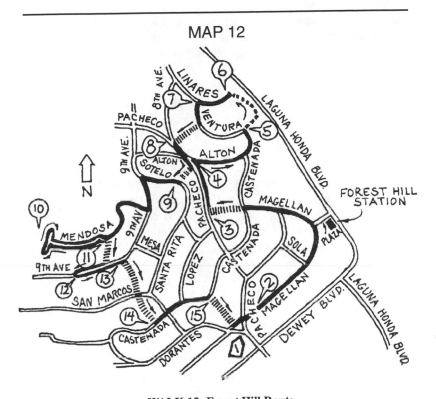

WALK 12: Forest Hill Route

Public Transportation: Muni L, M, or K Metro to Forest Hill Station. Right on Laguna Honda, Right on Dewey Blvd. to Magellan.

1. Begin at Magellan and Pacheco.
2. Right on Magellan to stairway next to No. 140 Castenada up to No. 334 Pacheco.
3. Right on Pacheco.
4. Right on Alton; left on Castenada to Ventura.
5. Next to No. 95 Castenada, go through open fence to footpath. Walk toward left.
6. Come out at cul-de-sac of Linares 080 & Ventura 000.
7. Left on Ventura. Ascend stairway next to No.20 Ventura to Pacheco (No. 452).
8. Left on Pacheco. Walk up 10 steps to upper Pacheco (near No. 400 Pacheco). Continue on Alton Stwy. next to No. 399 Pacheco.
9. At the top of stairway next to No. 60 Sotelo, bear right, then left on 9th, right on Mendosa.
10. Go to end of cul-de-sac to the left to see great view, and to the right to see ship-shaped houses. Make U turn.
11. Descend stairway next to No. 91 to upper 9th.
12. Curve around to right, then left on Lower 9th.
13. Descend stairway on lower 9th past San Marcos to Castenada.
14. Left on Castenada to Grand Stwy. next to No. 245.
15. Descend to Magellan and to our beginning.

urns, concrete benches, balustrades, parks and terraces. Forest Hill also has the distinction of having the largest concentration of Bernard Maybeck homes in the City. (He also designed the Clubhouse at No. 381 Magellan.)

No. 266 Pacheco was the first house built in Forest Hill (1913). In 1918, the year the first streetcar went through the Tunnel, the Forest Hill Association was organized. They set home-building standards such as a minimum 1,500-square-foot interior and 19-foot setback from the sidewalk. They taxed themselves in order to maintain the grounds; and since the streets and stairways, delightful and unconforming, did not meet city specifications, the Association was also responsible for them. After years of controversy and court action, the City accepted Forest Hill in 1978 as its responsibility, but did not begin work on the deteriorating streets until 1982. The Association is still a very active community group which meets regularly at the Forest Hill Clubhouse.

In the meantime, we call the stairway, the Grand Pacheco Stwy., linking it to an important adjacent street.

We begin at the intersection of Merced and Pacheco to view the fine planning north into Forest Hill and south into the Edgehill neighborhood (Walk 11) along the axis of the Pacheco Stwy.

■ Walk north on Pacheco to Magellan. Turn right on Magellan to ascend the stairway next to No. 140 Castenada, a Maybeck-designed house of 1924. The new owner, entranced with Maybeck's design, used the original construction style in remodeling the kitchen. We almost miss seeing the carved grape vines along the eaves. At the top we are at No. 334 Pacheco. We turn right.

At Alton Ave., turn right, then left on Castenada to Ventura.

No. 2 Ventura has a magnificent cactus garden that complements the southwest style of the house. Next to No. 95 Castenada we go through an opening in the fence to walk on a footpath on our left. We see below us Laguna Honda Blvd. and the reservoir.

We curve around and come out at the cul-de-sac of Linares 080 and Ventura 000.

Turn left on Ventura, and ascend the stairway next to No. 20, to No. 452 Pacheco.

Turn left on Pacheco. Ascend the 10 steps to upper Pacheco(near No. 400.) Continue on Alton Stwy., next to No. 399 Pacheco.

At the top of the stairway we are next to No. 60 Sotelo. (To the left at No. 51 is a 1914 Maybeck house with a curved off-center balcony, the sides decorated with an open carved-wood design.) Bear right then left on 9th, to go right on Mendosa. We follow Mendosa past Gateview Ct. to its

Pacheco Street

natural cul-de-sac. This extension of Mendosa was the last to be bull-dozed, and is now completely developed.

■ The hemispherical view from the point is a San Francisco special. The garden was designed by the neighbor who also placed the bench there for us to enjoy the scene. The sand is now covered and held by moss campion and daisies. Atmospheric conditions over the ocean discharge a translucent chiaroscuro over the City's hilltops and rooftops, and over the clouds themselves.

■ Moving away from this vista is one of the most difficult decisions we make on our walk, but there is contrast at the other end of the Mendosa cul-de-sac near the water-pumping station: two houses built in the shape of ships. Though there are several ship-shaped houses in San Francisco, these two are the most shiplike. I particularly enjoy their location at the edge of a precipice, where the captain might take a reading from the upper deck, with the Pacific Ocean practically in his front yard.

■ Return to Mendosa, and descend the stairway next to No. 91 to upper 9th.

■ Curve around upper 9th to lower 9th. Descend the stairway on lower 9th (next to No. 2238), past San Marcos to Castenada.

■ Left turn on Castenada. No. 270 is a 1918 Maybeck. It is a three-story, shingled residence with bays and dormers, and it feels as though it resisted mightily being confined within walls. Next to No. 245. is the Pacheco Stwy. As we descend the "Grand" Stwy. back to the street, we think of Jerry Healy, the first superintendent gardener of the tract (also called "Mayor of Forest Hill"). It was Healy who planted geraniums and marguerites so that the area was a mass of red and white colors.

■ We descend to Magellan to our beginning.

Walk 13

FOREST KNOLLS
Grading and Sliding

Forest Knolls neighborhood, on the slopes of Mt. Sutro, is built up on 10,000 years of layers of sand that have blown in from the beach, causing instability in times of earthquakes and heavy rains. It is bounded by 7th Ave. and the Sunset neighborhood on the west, and Clarendon Ave. and the Twin Peaks neighborhood on the east. It is a neighborhood where the fog settles in the tops of the eucalyptus, and the residents love the feeling of a non-urban atmosphere, while retaining the advantages of the City.

Mt. Sutro (elevation 908 feet) is composed mostly of red chert, the dominant rock in the Mt. Davidson/Twin Peaks area, and because it is one of the hardest ingredients of the Franciscan Formation, and little affected by wind and rain, it accounts for the high elevation in this part of the City. After a landslide occurred in the Forest Knolls neighborhood in 1966 (the area is underlain by dune sand and alluvial deposits), a building moratorium was declared for ten years. New homes have been built in the 1980s, necessitating expensive engineering.

■ We begin our walk at Oak Park and Forest Knolls, just off Clarendon. Turn left on Oak Park. Between Nos. 301 and 291 Oak Park is the Blairwood Lane Stwy. We walk up halfway, to Christopher. The plantings across the street are beautifully terraced with pines, eucalyptus, ice plants, century plants, and marguerites. To the right, the fog hangs in the eucalyptus trees on Mt. Sutro.

■ We turn left on Christopher, follow it to Warren, and turn right. The attractive, recently-built, single-family dwellings, pastel-colored and angled, thoughtfully allow for maximum light, both reflected and direct.

Across from No. 399, we ascend what I consider a floating stairway, hidden among the eucalyptus, the Oakhurst Stwy. The word "hurst," so often attached to English village names, means "wood".

Well, here we go, and we feel we are trudging through the opening scene of Charlie Chaplin's *The Gold Rush*. Instead of snow, a landscape of eucalyptus, bottlebrush, daisies, weeds, ice plants and mallow; instead of snow, the Pacific Ocean as far as the eye can see.

The climb is steep. Halfway up the zigzag stairway, we sit on the steps to admire an extraordinary wide-angle view. An ocean liner glides east; St. Anne's Church on Judah and Funston and the Public Health Hospital at 15th Avenue and Lake Street are visible through the fog.

But there are more steps to walk. Finally we are at Oak Park. Turn right into a narrow walkway that leads into the cul-de-sac. A series of new single-family dwellings have been built on our left. Nos. 560 and 550 were built in 1980, the others in 1990 and 1991. I-beams have been placed deep into the rock to provide safety for these homes, built in this landslide area.

We return to the stairs, and continue our ascent to Crestmont Dr. Across the street, a huge retaining wall delineates Sutro Woods development, Adolph Sutro's former hunting grounds. With the proceeds from the sale of his mine pump (designed to prevent flooding and the build-up of excess heat in the silver mines), Sutro, one of my favorite San Francisco pioneers, bought one- twelfth of San Francisco, and planted more than a half-million trees on his property.

Turn right. Many wild creatures must be enjoying concealment in the thick foliage as we pass by. At Crestmont and Devonshire, the fog is gaining on us rapidly. Each house on Crestmont has a garden reached via stairs. Between Nos. 95 and 101, closeby a white fire hydrant, is the Blairwood Lane Stwy.

We descend to Christopher and turn left. Just beyond the Glenhaven Lane Stwy., next to No. 191, we see the hillside rock formation, in colors from beige to red. As we walk down to Oak Park, we see a monkey-puzzle tree in the distance. We arrive at our beginning. Food is available in the Irving St. and Judah St. sections of the Sunset, or the Market St. and Castro St. sections of Upper Market.

Alternate: We can come in from the Sunset District at Lawton and 6th Ave., walk to Warren, turn right on Oakhurst Stwy. to Crestmont. Right on Blairwood Stwy. to Warren. Continue to Oak Park to Clarendon, an important corridor that can lead you to Twin Peaks or Upper Market or Forest Hill.

MAP 13

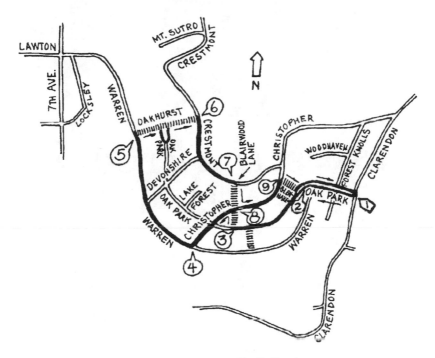

WALK 13: Forest Knolls Route

Public Transportation: Muni Bus # 36.

1. Begin at Oak Park and Forest Knolls Dr.
2. Bear left on Oak Park.
3. Ascend Blairwood Lane Stwy. to Christopher Dr., bear left.
4. Right on Warren to Oakhurst Stwy.
5. Ascend Oakhurst Stwy. Right into cul-de-sac of Oak Park. Return. Right on Oakhurst to Crestmont Dr.
6. Right on Crestmont to Blairwood.
7. Descend Blairwood Stwy. to Christopher.
8. Left on Christopher to Glenhaven.
9. Descend Glenhaven Stwy. to Oak Park to our beginning.

Walk 14

TWIN PEAKS & MT. SUTRO
At Last!

New York has its Statue of Liberty, Chicago has its Wrigley Building; Houston, its Astrodome, Seattle, its Space Needle, and San Francisco—its television tower on Mt. Sutro. We have seen it from different angles and from different locations throughout the City. Now we see this Sutro tower closeup and in full scale; we feel we are in the presence of the Golem, the frightening, fascinating, mechanical creature from Yiddish folklore, the prototype of Frankenstein's monster.

■ We begin our outing at Twin Peaks Blvd. and Mountain Spring. Walk up Mountain Spring. No. 32–34, the first house on the hill, occupies four lots, and was built in 1920, by the owner, who used handmade bricks. It is a multi-arched structure that overlooks a splendid view from the back of the house. Across the street is a contemporary home with clean lines and plain surfaces, which provide contrast and interest with the older homes.

■ We turn left to walk on Glenbrook. Crossing St. Germain, we discover that most of the homeowners here have installed large windows to partake of the magnificent views. Immediately ahead of us, across Palo Alto Ave., is the Sutro TV tower. It was originally designed to consolidate the many TV towers and antennae from the various channels. However, the closer one lives to it, the more problems one has with interfering radio frequencies and electronic hum and buzz. I know; I had to put my sound equipment in a steel enclosure.

■ Turn left to walk on Palo Alto Ave. A magnificent Monterey cypress grows in front of No. 160. We're above the fog line, with one of those

MAP 14

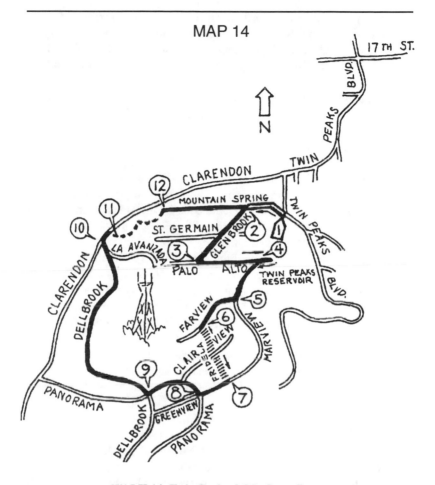

WALK 14: Twin Peaks & Mt. Sutro Route

Public Transportation: Muni Bus #37 and #33 run on Clayton.

1. Begin at Twin Peaks Blvd. and Mountain Spring. Walk west on Mountain Spring Ave.
2. Left on Glenbrook.
3. Left on Palo Alto Ave. Backtrack to Marview.
4. Left on Marview.
5. Right on Farview.
6. Left to Descend Fridela Lane Stwy. to Marview.
7. Right on Marview.
8. Right on Panorama.
9. Right on Dellbrook.
10. Right on Clarendon.
11. Walk on footpath across from No. 140 Clarendon to No. 136 Mountain Spring.
12. Walk on left side of Mountain Spring to Twin Peaks Blvd. to our beginning.

seductive views toward the north that residents say is their reward for the depression they suffer from continual summer fog. The house at No. 100 Palo Alto was the residence of Elmer Robinson, mayor of San Francisco from 1948 to 1956. The Twin Peaks Reservoir, 10 million-gallon capacity, just to our right, is used to charge the large blue-and red-topped hydrants that are part of the Fire Department's auxiliary water supply.

■ Backtrack on Palo Alto, and go left on Marview Way. We are traversing the Midtown Terrace neighborhood where Mt. Sutro abuts the backyards of the tract houses.

■ Right turn on Farview Ct. Next to No. 50 we make a left turn to descend the Fridela Lane Stwy. Along with a tall light standard, an unusual stairway feature, there is cypress, pine and a palm on the sides. The steep angle and high risers of Fridela remind us of the stairs to the Mayan Pyramids. We come to a walkway framed on each side by a house.

■ Cross Clairview Ct., and continue down the stairway to Marview. Turn right. Make another right on Panorama, and yet another right on Dellbrook, and walk on the even-numbered side that backs into Mt. Sutro. As we climb we become more aware of how close the hill is to the backs of the houses. We stand in front of No. 520, imagining how that canopy of mist hanging from the eucalyptus trees might affect us indoors. I would want to sit very close to a glowing fire.

■ We continue past La Avenzada, a private road that leads to the TV tower, and to Clarendon. At the crossroad with Dellbrook, we look to the left and see Christopher St., which leads to the Forest Knolls neighborhood (Walk 13).

■ From Dellbrook we turn right onto Clarendon. (Johnstone, the road that leads to UC housing for married students, is on the left).

■ We walk on the footpath across from No. 140 Clarendon and bear left up to Mountain Spring. We come out at No. 136 Mountain Spring. Walk on the left hand side of the street to see the views. The variety of architecture on the street is very pleasing to the eye, mainly because the height is uniform. We walk to Twin Peaks Blvd. to our beginning.

Walk 15

TWIN PEAKS, UPPER MARKET & IRON ALLEY
A Half-Cup of Tea

In the middle of the city is an outcropping of rock predominantly composed of chert, basalt, shale and sandstone. Man insisted upon streets, and the rock resisted; thus began a contest of angle vs. contour.

One outcome of this encounter is an inner area of enticing stairways that lead into other stairways. The short streets are in many ways comparable to those on the eastern side of the City. But the hills here are higher than Telegraph or Russian Hills, and the area was developed much later.

The Upper Market neighborhood is vast, full of nooks and crannies and small streets which curve beyond our sight into hidden stairways, high walls and precipitous gardens. It is becoming more interesting and better-known as an area of attractive, renovated Victorians and community gardens supervised by cooperative neighbors.

The Twin Peaks/Upper Market walk is akin to the White Rabbit's half-cup of tea. The other half is Walk 16, Upper Market/Bamboo and Lemons. If you would like to walk the two together as a single unit, it preferable to begin at Clayton and Iron Alley Stwy. (Walk 15).

■ We begin at Clayton and Iron Alley Stwy. (it is best to reach this place from Clayton rather than Market). The street sign at the corner says Clayton End and Market 3350. For some reason, the house next to Iron Alley Stwy. has a Market St. address—3304 and 3300.

■ Ascend the wooden stairs. (Don't forget to look back—the kinetic sensation I experience when I do is more pronounced and uncanny than

MAP 15

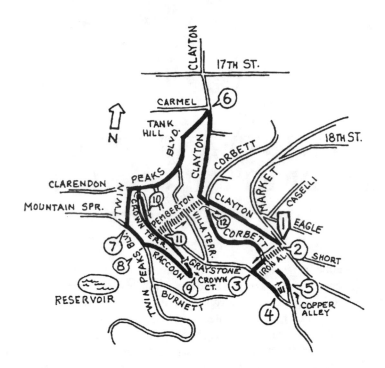

WALK 15: Twin Peaks, Upper Market & Iron Alley Route

Public Transportation: Muni Bus #33.

1. Begin at Clayton and Iron Alley Stwy.
2. Ascend stairway. Cross Corbett and continue to Graystone.
3. Left on Graystone.
4. Left on Copper Alley Stwy. Descend to Corbett.
5. Left on Corbett around bend, past Pemberton, to Clayton to Twin Peaks Blvd.
6. Left on Twin Peaks Blvd. Cross Blvd., Walk up stairs to see view from reservoir.
7. Return to other side of Blvd.
8. Turn left on Raccoon Dr.
9. Continue bearing left to Crown Ct. Continue left; cross over link chain. We are now on Crown Ter.
10. Continue toward end of Crown. Return to sign (130 Pemberton/98 Crown).
11. Descend Pemberton Stwy.
12. Right on Clayton to Iron Alley to our beginning.

from other stairways.) We quickly single out former St. Joseph's Hospital, Corona Heights and the Transamerica building.

■ Cross Corbett and continue in the macadam Iron Alley to Graystone, where we are at the base of Twin Peaks.

■ Turn left on Graystone, left again on Copper Alley Stwy., and descend the stairs to Corbett. We note the view through the fence next to No. 579 Corbett. (The odd-numbered side has the views.) Left on Corbett around the bend, past Pemberton, and onto Clayton. Continue on Clayton to Twin Peaks Blvd. and turn left onto the Blvd. Across the street is a short stairway to Water Dept. land where we can walk on the covered reservoir and view an unobstructed vista. Recross the Blvd. At the corner of Crown Terrace, we have a fine view of the contemporary house that was built according to code and in defiance of neighbor hostility. Turn left at Raccoon Dr.

Raccoon is an unusual access road—it has a spectacular view. Continue down to Crown Ct., where there are a few homes to the right. We go to the left and cross over a link chain (we are now on Crown Ter. The chain was put there to indicate the end of auto traffic from Crown Ct.).

The stone house on our left is uncommon and shy and perfectly fits into its cul-de-sac position. Crown Ter. is part of the section that was known in the 1930s as Little Italy—the Bank of Italy, now Bank of America, held many of the neighborhood's mortgages (and many of them were foreclosed during the Depression).

■ Continue to the end of Crown to enjoy the ambience, then return to the sign, 130 Pemberton Place/98 Crown Ter., to begin the descent on Pemberton Stwy.

■ I enjoy tracking changes in neighborhoods that I have been exploring over a period of years. When I go back over previous descriptions I feel I'm looking at a palimpsest. In 1981 I wrote of that wonderful feeling of luxury I felt the first time I descended the wide section of Pemberton. I imagined myself in fine velvet and lace, slowly descending the ballroom staircase from *War and Peace* to be swept into a sea of waltzers.

■ The heavy rains of 1982–83 precipitated the crumbling of brick stairs and the sandstone wall entrance along Clayton. The Department of Public Works installed 4x4 beams to prevent total collapse.

In 1991 I wrote that the support beams are still in place, and that we walkers are becoming inured to the dismal entrance to one of the most graceful stairways in the City.

■ It is 1995 and Pemberton Stwy. is in the process of being redesigned and newly landscaped.

Stamped concrete stairs, in a lovely shade of terracotta, are already in place between Graystone and Villa Terrace. A simple narrow handrail, Japanese maple at the landing, shade tolerant ground covers of vinca and jasmine, plus colorful annuals will return the area to its former grandeur for all pedestrians to enjoy.

■ The engineers and landscape architect, and others involved from the Department of Public Works, are enjoying the challenge of designing a new kind of stairway that meets the code requirements for safety, yet will reflect the architectural variety and the ambience of a cloistered area that still prevails on the hill. The spirit of community and team work between the department and the neighbors began with the patient and thorough neighborhood grass roots planning, spearheaded by one of the Pemberton residents.

■ Continue down past Graystone, past Villa Terrace, to Clayton.

■ From the entrance to the stairway on Clayton, turn right to walk to Iron Alley, to our beginning.

The Twin Peaks/Upper Market/Iron Alley walk is akin to the White Rabbit's half-cup of tea. The other half is No. 16, Upper Market/Bamboo and Lemons. If you would like to walk the two together as a single unit, start with Walk 15. When you come to Pemberton Stwy., (No. 11 on the route) walk down to Graystone, turn right onto Twin Peaks Blvd. to Clayton. Turn left to 17th to begin the Bamboo Walk. End the walk by turning left on Clayton from Corbett, to Iron Alley and our beginning.

Pemberton Place

Walk 16

UPPER MARKET
Bamboo and Lemons

If we were to walk from Ocean Beach at the western end of the City and finally arrive at 17th St. and Clayton, we could say we had worked up to it. After the flats, the land begins sloping upward toward 19th Ave. At about Fourth Ave. and Parnassus, where the University of California is, the altitude is noticeably higher.

At 17th and Clayton, we're even higher, entering a relatively unknown area where cut-off streets confuse, where there is no shopping, where urban walkers relish the exploring. A forty-year resident of Upper Terrace says when people realize how difficult it is to maneuver on the narrow street, they usually depart, leaving behind them privacy and quiet.

■ We begin near the intersection of 17th St. and Clayton. Cross over to the side of the street where there are new apartments on the corner, walk down 17th St. for 50 feet so that you can see the stilts on which the redwood shingle apartment complex is built, and also the Franciscan Formation that composes the hill. Return to the corner, and ascend the stairway on the north side of 17th St., a very abrupt, ambitious beginning, though the rise extends only from 449 feet to 476. Jade plants are growing along the stairway, but through the foliage we can see the Marin hills. At the top we are on Upper Terrace where multiple dwellings dominate the street.

■ Turn left toward Monument Way, which at one time marked the center of San Francisco. Bear to the right of the large, raised, concrete, circular, planting area in the center of the street, where pyracantha and Monterey cypress are growing. In 1887, Adolph Sutro placed the Olympus Monu-

90

ment here—a sculpture of a Greek goddess. If we ascend the stairs, we see that the pedestal is still present; the sculpture has been vandalized, and the 360-degree panorama of the City is partially concealed by shrubbery.

■ Next to No. 480 Monument, is Monument Stwy. which we descend to Upper Ter. Turn left. This is a pretty street; the quality of the light and the small distinctive houses make the area feel airy and inviting. We continue on Upper Ter. to Clifford Ter. Turn right at the bottom of the slope, walk down six steps, cross Roosevelt Way, and descend the Roosevelt Way Stwy.

■ We turn left on Lower Ter. This is it—one of the most impressive views in San Francisco, behind No. 54 Lower Ter., a Stick-style Victorian built in the late 1880s. Across the ravine is Corona Heights, 510 feet high, a jagged, stark hill of Franciscan Formation where new stairways have been installed; to the east, the Bay with container ships skimming by. It is a mesmerizing view.

■ Turn left on Levant. A few feet away, we turn right onto Vulcan Stwy., a miniature Shangri-La, where neighbors have traditionally worked together to beautify the gardens and walks. On one side is a sloping row of remodeled, eclectic, mostly wooden turn-of-the- century cottages. The flexibility of these early houses, whose new, well-designed patios, decks and skylights extend outdoor living to the interiors, is a marvel. An imposing, mature date palm stands one-fourth of the way down the stairway, and the scent of mock orange blossoms pervades the air. Cypress, eucalyptus, Scotch broom, fuchsia, rhododendron, azaleas, and hydrangeas are in full bloom. The datura, a plant from Peru, has giant, bell-shaped flowers. A living fence of bamboo obscures a thriving lemon tree in one of the yards.

■ At the bottom of the stairway we are on Ord St., where we turn right to the Saturn Stwy. and ascend. This planetary stairway has been recently redesigned by the Public Works Dept. after years of neglect. Except for the hand-rails, I like the pattern very much. I enjoy the contrast with Vulcan and the different mood it casts.

■ Visually directing us to the stairway are two, six-foot-wide patterned brick lanes on the sidewalk, and sweet fennel and overhanging cotoneaster shrubs on the retaining wall. On either side of the center plantings is a stairway—one built of railroad ties, and the other, of concrete. Benches have been positioned on raised brick and headerboard platforms for us to sit and enjoy the views, while being part of a green area planted with a redwood tree, acanthus, privit and agapanthus.

■ The top of the stairs brings us into the cul-de-sac of Saturn, a divided street where we walk on the upper level. The houses are small and the street feels cozy.

■ Bear left on Saturn to Temple St. Turn left on Temple. At 17th St. turn right, uphill to Uranus. Cross at the stop light here; turn left on 17th to Mars. There is a 17% grade on this thoroughfare, and we can appreciate the difference stairways make in navigating hills. I am including a small section on the south side of 17th so that we can better sense the contours of the land, and also walk by some older homes and cottages that have been here since the 1880s. This area is part of Eureka Valley neighborhood that has one of the oldest functioning community organizations in the City. During the decade of the 1980s, there was extensive renovation of the Victorian homes.

MAP 16

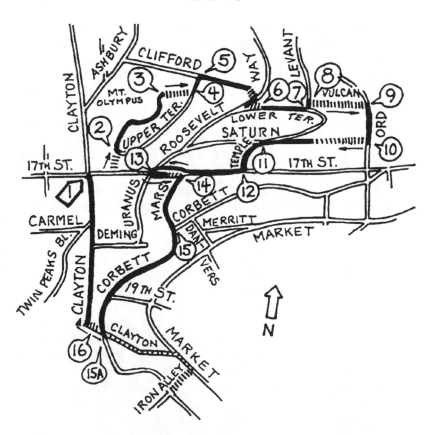

■ Turn right on Mars, and travel the higher side. Continue to Corbett, and turn right. Next to No. 367 at Mono is Al's Park complete with bench, bird bath, flowers, and a narrow dirt path that one can walk down to a fence at Market.

■ Bearing right, we come to Clayton. (In the first decade of 1900, the Mountain House Inn was here, and there was a wooden bridge over a water run-off originating from Mountain Spring.) Walk up the charming small stairway. The mini-garden on the side is another community project. Market St. is below us, the Sutro TV tower is to our left, and the view in back of us is worthy of a head turn. Continue on Clayton to 17th, walking on the right side for views of the Bay, to our beginning.

ADDENDA: If you are taking the complete walk (#s 15 and 16) and you begin with the Twin Peaks/Upper Market/Iron Alley walk, and wish to return to Iron Alley from the *Bamboo and Lemons* walk, turn left on Clayton (Circle #15) to Iron Alley.

WALK 16: Upper Market Route

Public Transportation: Muni Bus #33 Or#37 run on Clayton.

1. Begin at 17th and Clayton, ascend stairway to Monument Way.
2. Bear left and then right around Monument.
3. Next to No. 480 Descend stairway to Upper Ter.
4. Left on Upper Ter.
5. Right on Clifford Ter., descend six steps, cross Roosevelt Way. Next to No. 473 descend stairway to Lower Ter.
6. Left on Lower Ter.
7. Left on Levant.
8. Right on Vulcan to Ord.
9. Right on Ord to Saturn.
10. Ascend Saturn Stwy. to cul-de-sac.
11. Turn left on Temple.
12. Right on 17th to Uranus.
13. Cross 17th, left on 17th to Mars.
14. Right on Mars, walking on upper level to Corbett.
15. Right on Corbett to Clayton.
16. Right up stairs to Clayton. Continue right to beginning.

15A. Left on Clayton to arrive at Iron Alley if you are taking Walk 15 also.

Walk 17

CORONA HEIGHTS
Between the Houses

Corona Heights, one of San Francisco's 42 hills, is 510 feet high and very near the City's geographical center. From here, we have easy access to the neighborhoods south of Market Street via Castro and Clayton. This walk, with Walk No. 16, takes us on both sides of Corona Heights.

■ We begin at the intersection of Buena Vista Terrace and Roosevelt Way. As we walk downhill on the odd-numbered side of Roosevelt, we look at the Bay toward the east and the grand vistas of valleys and hills. Behind us is the large, handsome structure that formerly was St. Joseph's Hospital, now the 220-unit Park Hill condominiums. The houses on this block are well cared for; we see a lovely palm tree in the yard of No. 32 Roosevelt.

■ Across the street from No. 26 Roosevelt is the Henry St. Stwy. The stairway hillside is undergoing renovation, a cooperative effort among the neighbors, who initiated the process; the Department of Public Works who hauls away tremendous amounts of overgrowth; and San Francisco Beautiful who assisted with funds for plant materials.

■ Descending the stairway into the cul-de-sac, we walk past the back of McKinley School, a one-story building painted in shades of terracotta. There are three houses on the block that I think are significant—two flat, false-front Victorians at Nos. 215 and 213, and a pitched roof with a bay at No. 209.

■ Cross Castro St. (It is safer to cross at the stoplight one block to our left at 14th St.) There is also a fine corner grocery where we can buy trail nourishment. Continue to the right to Henry. The large structure at the

94

MAP 17

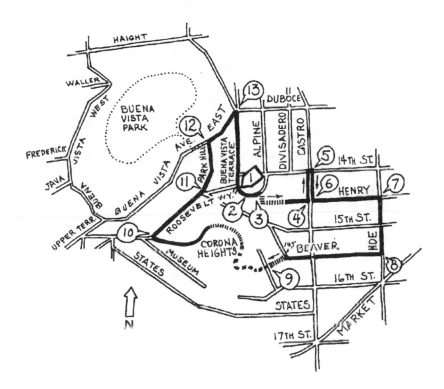

WALK 17: Corona Heights Route

Public Transportation: Muni Bus #37 stops here.

1. Begin at Roosevelt Way and Buena Vista Ter.
2. Walk downhill on odd-numbered side of Roosevelt.
3. Descend Henry Stwy. to Castro.
4. Left to 14th St. cross Castro.
5. Walk south to Henry.
6. Left on Henry to Noe.
7. Right on Noe to Beaver.
8. Right on Beaver. Next to No. 145 Beaver, ascend stairway into Corona Heights Park.
9. Follow path and stairways to Roosevelt.
10. Right on Roosevelt to Park Hill.
11. Left on Park Hill to Buena Vista East.
12. Right on Buena Vista East to Buena Vista Ter.
13. Right on Buena Vista Ter. to our beginning.

corner of Castro and Henry (Nos. 197–191) has an abundance of details to enjoy.

Turn left on Henry, and right on Noe. I particularly like this 100 block, not only because the Victorians are so well taken care of, but it is tree-lined with ficus and carob and Brisbane box trees, and has the feeling of a village street. A restaurant, a cleaners, a greengrocer, a flower shop, a guitar maker, all have their small establishments on this block.

Cross 15th St. and continue to the mini-park at the corner of Noe and Beaver, a felicitous space for friends and neighbors to meet and visit. Podocarpus trees in the raised planters, and benches and tables with permanent chess and checker boards enhance its use.

Turn right on Beaver, where again we see the synergistic effect of a fine asortment of Victorians with rectangular bays, and street trees. We are walking uphill. Note the special set-back, two-family home at Nos. 123–125 Beaver.

Next to No. 145 Beaver is the stairway we ascend. At the top, we are at the tennis courts of Corona Heights Park.

Go through the gate, and bear right going uphill. We are in back of the Junior Museum, dedicated to Josephine Randall,the first Superintendent of Recreation in San Francisco. She was able to fulfill her dream of establishing a nature museum which would instill in children a love of science, natural history and the arts. The Museum, in its present location since 1951, has been the source of inspiration and the initial training for many local people who have become well-known in various fields of natural history. A continual series of lectures, exhibits of geology and anthropology and classes in natural history, photography,ceramics and carpentry, plus a collection of small animals in the petting zoo make this a popular gathering place for adults as well as children.

At the fork in the road where the silver dollar eucalyptus tree stands, bear right on the new stairway, installed in 1990 to minimize erosion of the fragile hill, and to give the young native plants an opportunity to take root. Ahead of us is a startlingly beautiful panoramic view of the Bay and the hills, downtown San Francisco to the north, and to the south, Bernal Heights with the microwave station. We see McKinley School below us, with its striking blue trim and vents. Here we also derive a measure of our height. Continue looking to the left; where the stairway descends we see the remains of a brick structure. Rock climbers do practice their skill on top of Corona Hill, but we will continue on the path ahead of us.

Follow the path that is fenced on the right side. We come into a clearing and exit at the gate where the sign, Josephine Randall Museum, is on a standard.

■ We are at Museum and Roosevelt. (If you would like to visit the Museum, turn left on Museum Way for a short distance.) Turn right on Roosevelt. Note the lovely tuck-in at No. 284, the Victorians at Nos. 227 and 223. The new town houses across the street are in keeping with the ambience of the block, and the light color gives the street an added sparkle.

■ Continue across Roosevelt to Park Hill. No. 49 has a living arbor entrance to the front door, and a living fence.

■ At Buena Vista East, turn left to see the esthetic Park Hill condos. The panoramic view seen from the front glass door through the rear glass door is fully realized.

■ Buena Vista Park, across the street, is one of the oldest in the City—since 1870. It has paths, benches, many trees, and a variety of elevations, and many new stairways. It has been undergoing extensive renovation during an erosion-control and reforestation project. (If you have time, amble through now. Otherwise, I heartily recommend you make a special excursion to explore the park.)

■ Return to the corner of Park Hill and continue on Buena Vista East. At Buena Vista Ter., where we see the grand entrance to the park, turn right. Walk past 14th St. to our beginning.

Walk 18

EUREKA VALLEY
Amazing Footpaths

Eureka Valley encompasses the area below the southern slope of Twin Peaks. It is wedged between Diamond Heights, Noe Valley and Upper Market. It has one of the oldest continuously functioning neighborhood associations in the City.

Eureka Valley's Castro St. is the shopping center and the hub of the gay community, an important sociological and political force in San Francisco since 1970.

In 1977 Harvey Milk became the first admittedly gay member of the San Francisco Board of Supervisors. After his and Mayor George Moscone's murder in 1978 by a deranged former supervisor, Milk was replaced by another gay, Harry Britt, who has since been re-elected. The gay movement's militancy has created an awareness in the general public of procedures in the police department and in work-places that discriminate against gays and lesbians; it has also been effective in influencing the Board of Supervisors to pass the San Francisco domestic partners law which allows health insurance benefits for the partner of a City employee.

Castro Street supports a variety of boutiques, stores, restaurants and bars in addition to the Castro Theatre, a 1923 movie palace, where repertory films are exhibited, and where an organist plays the Wurlitzer before the first show, during intermissions and silent features.

The gay influence is apparent in many facets of street life: the concentrated number of skillful renovations of Victorian homes throughout the neighborhood; taxis always available; people commonly carrying bouquets of flowers—as gifts or for one's home; the Twin Peaks bar at Market—a durable and highly visible presence for 20 years; the Harvey

MAP 18

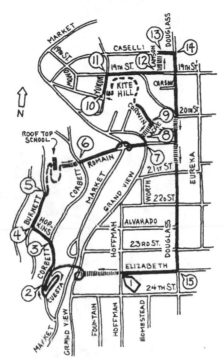

WALK 18: Eureka Valley Route

Public Transportation: Muni Bus #48 stops here.

1. Begin at Elizabeth and Hoffman. Ascend sidewalk stairway to Grand View. Walk on circular skyway that crosses Market St. to Corbett.
2. Left on Corbett to Cuesta Ct. Return to Corbett.
3. Left on Hopkins.
4. Right on Burnett.
5. Walk into common parking area at sign of Rooftop School. Continue to right through playground, bear left to descend stairway to Corbett.
6. Cross Corbett onto Romain, over the skyway to Grand View.
7. Left on Grand View.
8. Right into Acme Alley.
9. Left on Corwin to Kite Hill. Take footpath toward left. Descend stairway to Yukon.
10. Right on Yukon.
11. Right on 19th.
12. Next to No. 4612 descend Lamson Stwy. to Caselli.
13. Right on Caselli.
14. Right on Douglas.
15. Right on Elizabeth to our beginning.

Elizabeth Street

Milk Plaza and the Hibernia Bank Plaza where placards and sign-up sheets for various gay causes are circulated.

On Halloween, Castro Street bank tellers, clerks, and business people begin the day in a holiday spirit, wearing costume and make-up. In the evening the street between Market and 18th is blocked to auto traffic while *everybody* is out in full costume—elaborate, outrageous and colorful.

■ Our Eureka Valley walk, an eloquent cadence of repeated stairs, alleyways, views and skyways is an exploration of streets and parks behind the thoroughfares.

■ We begin at Elizabeth and Hoffman Streets and walk west on the (north) right hand side of the Elizabeth sidewalk stairway to Grand View Avenue. The houses, the flowers and trees and the stairway all seem to be in scale and in the right proportion to one another. We cross Grand View, bear right to the circular skyway over Market and continue onto the path to Corbett.

■ Turn left on Corbett and follow it into the lovely cul-de-sac of Cuesta, off Market and Corbett. There's a seven-step stairway from the street to the sidewalk, and another one from Cuesta to Market. We return to Corbett, bear right, and make a left on Hopkins. Lovely area but dismal architecture.

■ Turn right on Burnett. There are several levels to Burnett, but we stay on the first. We follow the street to the Rooftop School. Go into the driveway of a group of town houses, continue downward and around the back of the school, and through the playground. We go out from the left side of the yard, descending the stairway to Corbett. Meeting a neighbor who is waiting for the bus, we are informed that she has lived here since 1947, and still enjoys the area.

■ Cross Corbett to Romain. Pastel houses and a big view characterize this street. On the left-hand side is a series of bungalows dating from 1927. A resident who is gardening tells us he bought his house then for $15,000. It is now worth $400,000.

■ From the cul-de-sac, we walk over the skyway above Market St. and continue on Romain until Grand View, where we turn left.

■ Between Nos. 67 and 59 are three apartment houses, very nicely angled. They are built on the foundation of an older home. We turn right, descending Acme Alley (in the process of becoming a beautiful alley—I remember it when it was an eyesore.) A neighbor has installed brick and railroad-tie stairs and a lovely seat from railroad ties; espaliered bushes, trillium and a terraced fern garden; lilies of the Nile, rose bushes, lobelia, thunbergia and dogwood. The stairway will be extended to Corwin.

Turn left on Corwin, and at the end of the cul-de-sac, next to No.185, is a path to Kite Hill. It has been developed with Open Space funds; it is inviting and functional. Walkers use it; dogs and their owners use it. While sitting on the corner of a bench, I heard a lengthy discussion about dog personality types by a group of dog owners who were gossiping, while their charges were enjoying playtime.

Walk on the path on our right, veering toward the left (the views are always ahead of us). We come to a stairway that descends to Eagle. How delightful it is to walk into a park as easily as turning a corner. We turn right on Yukon, and right on 19th Ave. Next to No. 4612, we turn left to descend Lamson Ln. Stwy.to Caselli.

We proceed to our right. At No. 250 Douglass is Alfred "Nobby" Clarke's mansion, commonly known as Clarke's Folly, an officially-designated San Francisco landmark. Built in 1892 for $100,000, it tallied up five stories, 45 rooms, 52 closets, 10 fireplaces, 272 windows, plus towers and gables and chimneys.

Clarke was an Irish sailor who came to California in 1850. He made money by mining gold, then by becoming clerk to the police chief (supplementing by usury—$5.00 per month per $100 loaned), then by becoming a lawyer, then by becoming an entrepreneur (Clarke's Water Works). In 1904, eight years after Clarke went bankrupt, the structure became the California General Hospital. Today it consists of 15 one-bedroom apartments.

Turn right on Douglass which we follow to Elizabeth. The renovated turn-of-the-century homes at 20th are a great contrast to the ones built 30 years ago on Gardenside and Burnett. We ascend the Douglass Stwy. that curves gracefully between a house and garden on the left, and a hillside planted with cactus, bamboo and cypress, century plants and red hot poker.

Walk on the upper level of Douglass to enjoy a better view. The Alvarado Elementary School is at No. 625 Douglass. Through the initiative and leadership of sculptor Ruth Asawa, the school has received funds for an enriched art program over the past 20 years.

At the corner of 23rd, we look to the left to see a delightful series of four, false-front, rectangular-bay homes. When we stand in the middle of the street and look toward the west, we are in line with the middle of Twin Peaks. There was potential here for a beautiful corridor with a view.

Turn right at Elizabeth. Noe Ct. playground is equipped with childrens' play apparatus. Continue to Hoffman, to our beginning.

Walk 19

DOLORES HEIGHTS
A Mondrian Walk

A good walk is an organism of mysterious nuances that can affect us in subtle ways, from quiet harmoniousness to ebullience, from languor to exuberance. Within a walk for a stamp, a loaf of bread, a bit of exercise or a breath of fresh air, are the promising ingredients of an imaginative walk that charms and delights: the various terrain to step over, the spectrum of sky colors to see, the views of manufactured objects to comprehend, the assortment of people to meet, and the intrinsic rhythm and shape of the walk to sense.

I love to trace out the shape of a walk on paper after I walk it. I want to know if there is a correlation between the shape and how it feels when I walk; there is. For some reason that I don't understand, my early walks usually traced into the shape of a foot or a shoe, and the walks felt very comfortable. Now my walks seem to form fanciful figures, or geometric, Mondrian configurations, and they feel effortless. The Dolores Heights walk is Mondrian choreography!

■ We begin at 19th and Sanchez. Ceonothus, bottlebrush, and acacia grow at the base of the imposing wall that is the entry to double stairways going up Sanchez. (The first inspection is recorded in 1939.) We ascend the left stairway, and at the top, in front of No. 615, are four cypress trees, over 50 years old. At one time, Sanchez had brick paving, but it was too slick, and had to be covered with asphalt.

■ Passing Cumberland, we notice the extraordinarily beautiful pine at the corner. (I might as well confess now that the intersection of Cumberland and Sanchez is one of my favorite corners in San Francisco.)

We continue walking on Sanchez and we can see below us one section of the Cumberland Stwy. that goes down to Church. In front of No. 655 Sanchez, we descend the stairs to walk on the pedestrian walkway. We are walking south toward 20th St. on the lower part of the divided street. A center strip of plantings and unusual tilted stairs divides the upper and lower parts of Sanchez. The cul-de-sac of Sanchez angles to the left. We ascend the stairway to our right that brings us to the upper level of Liberty and Sanchez.

Cross Sanchez to continue up the Sanchez Stwy. which is fronted by a high retaining wall. When we look east toward our left we see the dome of the Christian Science temple on Dolores St. The house on the corner, No. 746 Sanchez, conforms to the irregular-shaped lot in a very comfortable way. Redwood-shingled, the house stretches around the corner, the off-front, arched veranda or possibly car port (although there is a garage off to the side), leading the eye to the terraced garden where camellias and a mature Douglas fir are the dominant plantings.

Continue to 21st St. The house at the corner, No. 3690, formerly belonged to "Sunny Jim" Rolph, the popular San Francisco mayor (1912–1931). The Monterey pine trees around the house were planted by John McLaren, who was the superintendent of Golden Gate Park for 60 years.

We are walking toward Hill St., formerly called "nanny goat hill", in reference to the goats who grazed here, and we enjoy a beautiful view to the south. At the turn of the century, the designated voting place for the neighborhood was a small structure on the top of the hill to our right. The house presently there is built across two city lots. Before the streets were paved, the firemen who were attached to the 22nd St. firehouse between Sanchez and Noe, (now a residence), left their pumps up here on the hill as a kindness to their horses.

There are many springs in the area. It is said that the Native Americans who lived near Mission Dolores came up here to get their water. There are still some houses around that have their own capped wells.

Historically, working-class people have resided in Dolores Heights, but now many professional people live here, and the mix is enriching the neighborhood. The residents love the sunny, fog-free weather.

We are on Hill and Sanchez. Look to the left to get the full measure of the elevation.

We reverse our direction and go back on Sanchez, turn left on 21st, and right on Rayburn, which takes us out to Liberty. A left turn brings us to the Liberty Stwy. which we descend to Noe.

The four white stucco, Art Deco houses alongside the stairway are foils for the multitude of Victorians in this neighborhood, from elaborate

MAP 19

WALK 19: Dolores Heights Route

Public Transportation: Muni Metro J runs on Church with stops on 18th and 20th; walk to Sanchez.

1. Begin at 19th St. and Sanchez. Ascend Sanchez Stwy. to Cumberland; descend small stairway to lower Sanchez; return to Upper Sanchez via stairway; cross St. Ascend stairway from Liberty to 21st. Continue to Hill St.
2. Return on Sanchez to 21st.
3. Left on 21st to Rayburn.
4. Right on Rayburn to Liberty.
5. Left on Liberty. Descend stairway to Castro.
6. Left on Castro to 22nd.
7. Right on 22nd. Ascend stairway to Collingwood.
8. Right on Collingwood to 21st.
9. Right on 21st. Descend sidewalk stairway to Castro. Continue to Noe.
10. Left on Noe to Cumberland.
11. Right on Cumberland. Ascend stairway to Sanchez.
12. Left to descend Sanchez Stwy. to 19th to our beginning.

Sanchez Street

Queen Annes of the late 1880s and 1890s to one-story flat-front Italianates of the 1870s and early 1880s.

■ While walking in the neighborhood, I am captivated by the constantly shifting cloud cover playing with the TV tower on Mount Sutro, obscuring it in one moment, uncovering it in the next. Sometimes we see the entire structure, sometimes just a part. At the moment we can see almost all of it.

■ Walk on the left (south) side of Liberty. A scooped skyline to the north, Corona Hill, and Buena Vista condos to the west, and the financial district highrises toward the east, come into focus; and in close-up, a plane tree in front of No. 521 Liberty, and a mature hibiscus across the street. Nos. 546–72 Liberty were built in 1897 by Fernando Nelson, a prolific developer of tract Victorians in this and other neighborhoods of the Mission. His houses display his favorite wooden embellishments: decorative circles and pendants which he called, "donuts" and "drips."

■ Continue on Liberty. As we approach Castro, our view of the Sutro tower has been reduced to the top third.

■ We turn left onto Castro. Queen Anne row houses are on the west side of the 700 block of Castro. Walk to 22nd St. and turn right. This section of 22nd is a turnabout with a sculptural, high-curved retaining wall that encompasses the stairway we ascend to Collingwood. (The stairway on the other side goes down to Diamond.) We're at the top of the hill of this five-block-long street.

■ Turn right on Collingwood. In 1932, a German mason built No. 480, a cobblestone house, using stones from the dismantled Castro cable car line. Turn right on 21st, which used to be extremely steep from Diamond to Castro. In 1924, the City "improved" the street by lowering the grade on one side and raising it on the other, resulting in a grade-separated street. The consequence was some non-usable garages. No. 3937's was converted into living space. Walk down the sidewalk stairway on the odd-numbered side of 21st and continue to Noe. The 3800 block of 21st has an exceptional selection of Queen Anne Victorians. On the left side, they gently follow the slope of the hill. Nos. 3816–36 are row Queen Annes, built by John Anderson, a contractor, in 1903 and 1904.

■ Turn left on Noe. At Liberty and Noe, we look up to the right, and see the stairway we had descended. From the odd-numbered side we see a scooped skyline to the north. Corona Hill and former St. Joseph's Hospital are to the west, and the financial district highrises are toward the east.

■ Note the amalgam at No. 763 Noe, on the right side. At 20th and Noe we pass a narrow stairway alongside the apartment house. The houses on the even-numbered side of the street have the potential of becoming a showcase similar to the homes on Alamo Square or on Clay St. across from Alta Plaza Park. Three-quarters of the ubiquitous Sutro tower is still in sight.

■ We ascend the Cumberland Stwy. across from No. 670 Noe. The retaining wall, made from cobblestones, is a backdrop to the outcropping of rock upon which the stairway was built. Several century plants, set into the rock soil, form a strong upright profile against the jumbled Franciscan Formation. Sedum, gazanias and ivy are growing here and there.

■ The cul-de-sac entrance at the top of the stairs begins a pleasant walk alongside tree-lined houses. No. 367 has an octagonal belvedere, roofed in a pattern of blue and lavender tiles. In the cobblestone terrace of No. 338 Cumberland, gold fish are swimming in the pond. The exterior of No. 333, a recent addition to the street, is cement composition board, a relatively new material that is just beginning to be used in San Francisco. The house provides contrast and a key to tracing the development of the neighborhood. No. 332 is a simple Craftsman-style house.

■ We continue to Sanchez, arriving at our favorite corner of Cumberland; turn left and descend the Sanchez Stwy. to our beginning. Eating places and stairway extensions surround us on Castro, on 18th, and on Market.

Walk 20

BERNAL HEIGHTS EAST
Stairway Trails

East Bernal Heights is above a vertical, crazed network of overpasses and underpasses which telescopes the history of San Francisco and Bay Area transportation.

The Ohlone Indians are the earliest settlers of the Bay Area of whom we have records. They moved about finding the best areas for fishing, hunting, and gathering acorns and plant foods. They managed to live adequately until the sixteenth century, when the Spanish and the English began arriving in ships and exploring the ocean and the coast. In the eighteenth century, the Catholic padres came north from Mexico, establishing missions along the road that became El Camino Real. Now Highway 82 faithfully follows most of this historic path, including the upland winter route around Alameda de las Pulgas in San Mateo County, which avoided the wet and muddy flatlands.

The Gold Rush of 1849 strained all modes of transportation into the city: ferry boats transported men and goods between San Francisco and the North and East Bays; horses and carriages, then trains, carried passengers from San Francisco south.

In 1926, the City began a search for an airport site when the U. S. Post Office awarded contracts to private individuals for delivery of air mail.

In 1927, Mills Field was dedicated as San Francisco's municipal airport. Some people still remember Mills Field as a favorite spot for watching pilots take off in their two-seaters to perform daredevil stunts. In 1930, the city bought all of the Mills estate, over a million acres, for development as an air terminal.

MAP 20

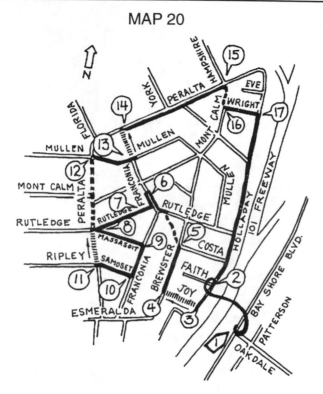

WALK 20: Bernal Heights East

Public Transportation: Muni Bus #23, #9.

1. Begin at Old Bayshore and Oakdale on west side of street. Walk on skywalk to Holladay.
2. Left on Holladay to Joy.
3. Right on Joy Stairway to Brewster.
4. Right on Brewster to Costa.
5. Walk on footpath toward left to Rutledge.
6. Right on Franconia. Return.
7. Right on Rutledge.
8. Sharp left on Massasoit.
9. Right on Franconia.
10. Right on Samoset.
11. Right to descend Peralta Stwy. and footpath to Mullen.
12. Right on Mullen.
13. Descend stairway to Peralta.
14. Right on Peralta, past York, past Hampshire.
15. Right on footpath to Montcalm.
16. Left on Wright.
17. Right on Holladay to our beginning.

As tourism increased, the stable population also grew. Bayshore Highway was dedicated in 1929. Heavy industry began moving into South San Francisco; World War II accelerated the movement of men and machines, super Highway 101 was built in the late 1940s and Highway 280 in the 1950s.

Major thoroughfares Alemany, Mission and Army crisscrossed and the area became a tangle of interlocking highways, each more super than the last, discouraging timid pedestrians from trying to find a way through the twentieth-century maze.

Bernal Heights, high above the maze, is part of the Rancho de las Salinas y Potrero Nuevo, granted to Jose Cornelio de Bernal in 1839, by the Mexican government.

In the 1860s, the rancho—one league square, approximately 4,000 acres—was subdivided, and Vitus Wackenreuder made a survey of Bernal Heights. Wackenreuder plotted his streets narrow and his lots small—23 by 76 feet. Most of them do not meet city specifications of minimum size. The east slope exceeds 45 percent grade in many places, and its geological composition has hazardous landslide potential.

After subdivision, the first group of settlers was predominantly Irish. They farmed the land and engaged in dairy ranching, the first extensive industry in Bernal Heights. Wakes were the most popular social gatherings, along with the telling of stories by "them as had the gift." The day Widow O'Brien's best milch cow was taken to the city pound, and all her neighbors helped her get it back was a true neighborhood story, endlessly told.

German and Italian settlers followed the Irish. During World War II, there was an influx of people, mainly blue-collar, from all over the United States, who came to work in the nearby naval shipyards.

More recently professional people have been moving into the neighborhood, attracted by the sunny climate and the neighborhood ambience of the village within the City. Since 1995, Bernal Heights East has experienced fundamental and dramatic changes. Sales tax monies have now made it possible to implement mandated life safety codes. Wood timber and concrete stairs, metal railings and wood deck landings, lights and landscaping have replaced higgledy-piggledy stairs and slippery slope trails. The new stairways at Brewster, Mayflower, Joy, Faith, and Rutledge provide access to new streets—wide and paved. All this construction, including the approved underground utilities for the East Slope of Bernal Heights, was coordinated by Peter Albert of the Department of City Planning. The East Slope is now one grand forest of stairway trails to explore. I encourage you to explore new routes and let me hear about your best ones.

We begin our walk on the west side (even numbered) of Bayshore Blvd. at Oakdale; walk north to the end of the block, then turn left to ascend Faith pedestrian overpass, a testimonial to grassroots action by Bernal Heights residents who fought for access across the freeway.

As we climb up to Holladay, we are aware of the noise level of traffic that rises and falls.

We turn left on Holladay and right on Joy at the craggy, corkscrew, willow tree. Ascend Joy Stwy. in the open hilly field planted with new live oak trees. Sitting to the left is a sculpture supported by wires, near the front of the house. Ahead of us are geraniums, lupins, poppies, and two healthy pines.

We continue up the wood stairs alongside Nos. 16, 18 and 20 Joy. All are originally flat-front Italianates from the 1870s and 1880s and have been remodeled in a variety of ways.

The fragrance of the salvia near No. 18 intensifies the feeling that we are walking on private grounds. Everything feels rural—a hidden urban treat.

We follow along wood steps past No. 20 to Brewster—just below the community gardens—and turn right. Then we walk on the footpath toward the left to Rutledge.

Right on Franconia to the landing next to No.233. The stairway is precipitous and unsafe, and the view is great. From east to west we see San Francisco General Hospital, the Tischman Building at 525 Market St., the darkly-colored Shaklee Building, Coit Tower, and former St. Joseph's Hospital near Corona Heights.

We return to walk right on Rutledge. No. 210 Rutledge has almost the same beautiful view through the window as we saw from the "corner." Rutledge is a tree-lined, charming, non-conforming street.

We make a sharp left on Massasoit (named for the 17th century American Indian chief of the Wampanoag tribe from Rhode Island. He was a great friend of the British, and sold them Duxbury). Right on Franconia to view the industrial scene of San Francisco and the East Bay.

We turn right on Samoset, (there seems to be a confluence of American Indian names that are interconnected: Samoset (1590–1653) was a leader of the Algonquins, spoke English, signed deeds and sold 12,000 acres to the Puritans. He also introduced Massasoit to the Puritans.

Turn right again on Peralta. Here at the "corner" is the Peralta Stwy. and the super-grand view of all. Today the light is perfect. We see Twin

Peaks and the Mt. Sutro TV tower to the west, Golden Gate Bridge and Mt. Tamalpais to the north, Angel Island and Coit Tower farther east.

■ We descend to Rutledge, which has an especially interesting assortment of flat-front structures in differing states of repair, and a large trailer with a roof sculpture. It moves, it stretches. Aha! It's a live goat!

■ No. 290 Rutledge is a visually-arresting home built by the architect-owner who deliberately sited the house on the southwest corner to utilize passive solar energy.

■ Continue down the footpath to Montcalm. No. 300 is a delightful 1906 cottage that has been tastefully renovated by the owners. They also have designed a garden containing lamb's ears, dusty miller, Atlantic blue cedar and Australian tea trees as well as annuals, along the footpath. It's difficult to imagine Peralta ever turning into an auto road.

■ Continue down the footpath to Mullen (Mullen 100 Peralta 200). Make a right turn on Mullen, which is now a divided street, upper and lower. At Franconia turn left to descend the stairway to Peralta. Turn right. Peralta is wide, there are several empty lots, and the houses are bigger.

■ At Peralta 100 York 1600, continue toward the left on Peralta. We see a good stand of large row Queen Annes. We are walking on the upper level. Across from No. 51 we see the Potrero thoroughfare and San Francisco General Hospital. Pass Hampshire. Walk on the footpath to our right that goes to Wright Pl., a neighborhood footpath. At Wright and Montcalm, we turn left on Wright and continue to Holladay.

■ We glance over to our left and see the remains of the Eve Stwy. and Adam Stwy. which disappeared when the freeway was built. At No. 118 Holladay someone painted a cow on the fence.

■ Turn right on Holladay, continue past York, Rutledge and Costa. The stairway at No.19 Rutledge is another new wood stairway that goes up to Mullen. We go onto the skywalk at Faith, and descend to our beginning.

Walk 21

BERNAL HEIGHTS WEST
Summer, Fall and Late Spring

Bernal Heights neighborhood is a benign sun pocket. It is bounded by four broad and busy thoroughfares—the Bayshore Freeway on the east, Mission St. on the west, Army St. on the north and Alemany on the south. The rancho of almost 4,000 acres was granted by the Mexican government to Jose Bernal in 1839. Francois Pioche, a banker, bought it in the 1860s and subsequently subdivided it. The rancho was used mainly for grazing of cattle and goats, truck farms and dairy farms.

Many of the Bernal Heights street names have Civil War associations—Banks, Winslow, Putnam, Army, Moultrie, Sumter. Eugenia, however, was named for the daughter of a tollkeeper on San Bruno Road.

■ We begin on Coso Ave. and Coleridge. Several Queen Anne rowhouses on the east side are newly painted. The Stick style at No. 130 Coso, which also bears the address of No. 1 Lundys Lane, has a corner rectangular bay window. Behind it, at No. 9 Lundys Lane, is an Italianate flat-front, positioned strangely—its side faces the street.

■ We walk up the Coso sidewalk stairway on the left-hand side of the street; veer to the left on Aztec and descend the stairway to Shotwell. Nos. 1429 and 1435 Shotwell were bonus plan cottages. These were available to 1906 earthquake victims who lost their homes, but still retained their jobs.

■ Turn right on Stoneman, cross the street, and we're at the foot of Bernal Hill, one of the City's 42 hills. The 23 acres of hilltop are under the jurisdiction of the Recreation and Park Department. The hill has been designated "a natural area in perpetuity." It is to be restored with plants

114

indigenous to the area. The Native Plant Society and the Bernal Heights Open Space Committee have been diligent in holding work parties to collect seed from the hill, and to plant bunch grass in test plots.

■ We follow a dirt path up the hill (to minimize erosion, stairs will probably be placed here). The hill, which is blocked off from vehicular traffic, is a pleasant place for walking, jogging, and bicycling. When we arrive at the top we have a choice of directions. If we go to the left, we almost cover the mile-long route around the hill, in addition to seeing an exquisite panoramic view of the city. (In 1876, there was a rumor of gold quartz in the hill.)

■ We decide to take the more direct route and turn to our right. Shortly, we come to the Esmeralda Stwy., which we descend.

■ The area surrounding the stairway has been gardened and cared for by several neighborhood gardeners who love plants and trees and Bernal Heights, and do all they can to create a beautiful environment. In the center of the planting area is a stone memorial and a California live oak dedicated to Margaret Randolph, neighborhood activist who organized the first Northwest Bernal Heights Club.

■ Red-hot poker grows nearby. A kestrel flies above us as we descend, probably looking for grasshoppers.

■ Left turn on Elsie. The street had been graded in an unconventional manner—it still has bumps and ridges and unevenness which actually create a more vivid contour portrait of the street. (I don't know how efficient the drainage is.) New housing has been built on the odd-numbered side—Nos. 139–173, in a very pleasing contemporary style with bay windows. No. 179 is a redwood-shingled house with a lovely curved stairway to the door.

■ We come to a quasi-triangular section of well-kept homes. The writing in the concrete says Virginia Ave. Continue, and turn right on Eugenia. From Winfield we descend the very pleasant stairway to Prospect. Bollards and greenery on both sides of the stairs are a charming announcement of a special pedestrian right-of-way.

■ Left turn on Prospect. The sign says, Prospect 326 and Kingston End. Across from No. 320, we descend the curved, floating Kingston Stwy. A striking rock formation on the left-hand side and a sign at the bottom of the stairway says, Kingston Gardens.

■ Turn right on Coleridge. This block has predominately multi-family dwellings. We go right on Eugenia and see eucalyptus, mirror plant, ivy and fuschia cascading over the wall, and flowering fruit trees. Left turn on Prospect where we walk downhill, past Heyman to Virginia; turn right. No. 201 at the corner is a fish-scaled, gabled, with bowed bays. (Unfortunately, the new windows in the bays are rectangular with aluminum frames.) No. 217 is a beautiful three-story Stick. We turn left on Winfield. No. 140 has a drawbridge. No. 119, a flat-front gabled, has charm and simplicity.

■ At Esmeralda turn left to descend the angled stairway to the viewing platform where we can see Twin Peaks. There are picnic tables, a sunken and trellised planting area with rosemary growing over the side, and slides in the playground. The annual Easter egg hunt takes place here. The behind-the-scene-work is a year-round cooperative activity of dedicated parents who save and color the empty eggshells, place toys into them, cover them with colored tissue and hide them.

■ The stairway begins again at Lundys. No. 100 on the left side is appealing. We continue down the stairway—enhanced by plantings of ceonothus, sage, and daisies on both sides, to Coleridge where the architectural device of bollards herald "A Stairway".

MAP 21

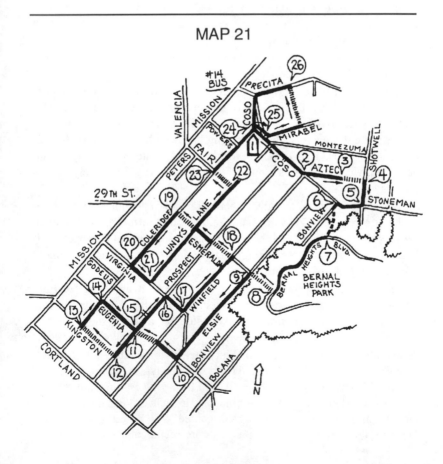

■ Left on Coleridge where we pass a mix of houses. No. 190 Coleridge is the Senior Citizen Housing put up by the Bernal Heights Community Foundations in 1989. This pleasingly executed building houses 190 seniors. A toddlers' playground near the entrance is well-utilized. The street trees are ficus.

■ Left on Virginia to a block lined with eucalyptus trees and left on Lundys Ln. The street carob trees, and the similar height of the homes, mostly from the 1880s and 1890s, bestow an ambience of continuity and charm. At this time we pass two empty lots, full of fennel and stork's bill;and a row of Queen Annes and flat-fronts. Walk past Esmeralda. The colors may be changed at any moment but at the present writing, No. 57, a flat-front Victorian, is multi-hued—orange, robin's-egg blue, dark blue, white. There are some very nice gardens on our left. At the cul-de-sac we are at Lundys and Fair. The house on our right, No. 17 is one of the oldest

---

WALK 21: Bernal Heights West Route

Public transportation: the #14 Mission bus stops at Mission & Precita. Walk to Precita, veer to the right on Coso.

1. Begin at Coso and Coleridge.
2. Walk south on Coso. Veer left on Aztec.
3. Descend Aztec Stwy. to Shotwell.
4. Right on Shotwell.
5. Right on Stoneman.
6. Left turn on Bonview. Slight left up footpath on hill to Bernal Heights Blvd.
7. Right on Bernal H. Blvd. to Esmeralda Stwy.
8. Descend.
9. Left on Elsie.
10. Right on Eugenia. Descend stairway to Prospect
11. Left on Prospect.
12. Right on Kingston. Descend stairway to Coleridge.
13. Right on Coleridge.
14. Right on Eugenia.
15. Left on Prospect.
16. Right on Virginia.
17. Left on Winfield.
18. Left on Esmeralda Stwy. to Coleridge.
19. Left on Coleridge.
20. Left on Virginia.
21. Left on Lundys Lane.
22. Left on Fair. Descend stairway to Coleridge.
23. Right on Coleridge.
24. Right on Coso.
25. Left on Mirabel. Next To No. 9, descend stairway to Precita.
26. Left on Precita. Left on Coso to Coleridge to our beginning.

Shotwell Street

in Bernal Heights, and is on its original homestead goat farm. It has been extended from a simple, gabled, thin clapboard to a roomy, two-story, eight-room structure. The front is No. 34 Prospect.

■ Walk to the right, to the end of Lundys cul-de-sac to look across the street to No. 23 Prospect, an architect-designed house that features an outsized front window and unusual interior lights

■ We return to the cul-de-sac to descend the Fair Stwy. down to Coleridge. To our right is the vegetable garden that neighborhood children have been working on under the supervision of community leaders.

■ We turn right on Coleridge to Coso, then right on Coso to Mirabel. Next to No. 9 we descend one of the narrowest stairways in the City, from Mirabel to Precita. Since No. 189, the house with the Beatles imagery, has been repainted, turn left on Precita to Coso and Coleridge, to our beginning.

Walk 22

EXCELSIOR
How Many Angles to a Block?

Where can you wait for someone at the corner of Naples and Italy; Moscow and Russia; Munich and Brazil; or Edinburgh and Persia? In the Excelsior neighborhood of San Francisco.

One of nine distinct neighborhoods of the Mission District, it is located in what is known as the Excelsior Homestead Tract, created in 1869, when the area was designated as urban farmland. Its boundaries are Geneva Ave., Alemany Blvd., Silver Ave., Madison St. and McLaren Park.

Excelsior was originally settled by Italian truck farmers who lived in small turn-of-the-century houses; Irish, who predominately became City employees; and Germans, who operated many delicatessans. After the 1906 earthquake, many homeless came here, and the area became a blue-collar neighborhood. After World WarII, Blacks moved here, then after the Vietnam War, Filipinos. Now the majority of newcomers in the neighborhood are Latinos from Central America. They and the Asians make up 50% of the Excelsior population. The other 50% is mostly older Europeans.

Early Excelsior was dotted by gardens and water towers and windmills. Corpus Christi Church, originally a National Italian Church (on our route), was founded by the Salesian Brothers in 1898. (They also established Sts. Peter and Paul Church in North Beach to serve the large number of Italian fishermen and day laborers in that neighborhood.) Mission St. was—and still is—the main business street of the Excelsior. Sorrento Deli still retains some of the early Italian flavor. The Ocean Railroad ran on what is now Alemany Blvd.; the Southern Pacific, on San Jose Ave. One could cross over to neighborhoods on the western side via Ocean Ave. and Monterey Ave.

The first time I looked westward from the heights of Excelsior onto Alemany and San Jose superhighways and #280, my reaction was "I'm trapped". I could not see any physical pedestrian access across the highways. I realize that visually it is important to see people walking across the streets.

The Excelsior walk is dramatic: it makes us aware of how freeways ringing a neighborhood can affect it; at the same time, it provides an antidote to the freeway auto maze/craze; it jolts our imagination backward to early Excelsior (we will see remnants); and it awards us with a challenging terrain and beautiful, unfamiliar views. The Excelsior walk is a strenuous one; we would suggest a snack and liquid; for the views, binoculars and a camera.

■ We begin at the Excelsior branch library at Mission and Cotter, an important institution in the neighborhood. The staff is bilingual, the chief librarian,known as an out-reach librarian, helps new immigrant-residents with their English, with insurance, Social Security and job application forms, in addition to normal librarian duties. Recent budget cuts have decreased the the extra services and library hours. The Excelsior library has two unusual collections: 600 books in the Spanish language and 500 books from the Philippines.

■ We go left on Mission toward Silver and turn right. At the corner, in a series of low brick buildings amid extensive grounds bordering on Lisbon St.,is the Jewish Home for the Aged, built in 1923. The landscaping is very attractive, soothing and comforting to the residents of the home— Jewish elderly who cannot manage on their own. JHA is a skilled nursing, long-term-care facility. It offers an excellent art and ceramics program; classes in current events, religion, and music; fine dental and medical care and short-term psychiatric care.

■ Continue on Silver, turn right on Madrid and walk on the even-numbered side to better view the rise toward our right, and a series of six pitched-roof Victorians on the odd-numbered side in various stages of decline.

■ Turn left on Peru. When we look back we see the row of pine trees on the grounds of the Jewish Home; toward the west we see the TV tower, Diamond Heights, and a little bit of the Mt. Davidson Cross. Looking toward our right we see the highrises of downtown San Francisco, and the microwave station on Bernal Heights. The small homes across the street are renovated in many different styles.

MAP 22

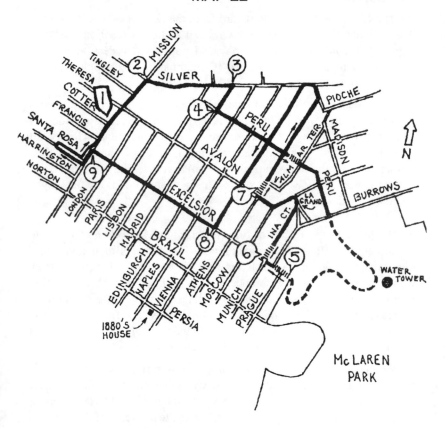

WALK 22: Excelsior Route

Public Transportation: Muni bus #22.

1. Begin at the library at Mission and Cotter. Walk on Mission in the direction of Avalon.
2. Right on Silver Ave. to Madrid.
3. Right on Madrid to Peru.
4. Left on Peru past Athens, to ascend stairway. Continue to Burrows. Follow footpath through McLaren Park toward right.
5. Descend Excelsior Stwy. to Munich.
6. Ascend Munich Stwy. to Ina Ct. Continue right on La Grand, left on Avalon to Athens.
7. Right. Ascend Athens Stwy. Continue on Athens, left on Silver. Left on Vienna to Excelsior.
8. Right on Excelsior to Mission.
9. Left on Mission, right on Santa Rosa to see Church. Return to Mission, left to Cotter to our beginning.

■ The mystery house on the corner of Naples looks very strange. The stairway leading to the door has been dismantled, windows have been boarded up, there is no visible entrance to the house, and a section of living space has been added to the structure. Neighbors say this has been the condition of the house for at least 20 years. The tuck-in at No. 410 Peru has a lovely front garden.

■ One of the neighbors who has lived in his house for 50 years remembers the Southern Pacific train that rode along what is now San Jose Ave.; he remembers Peru when it was bare from Vienna to the hill. One of the most important changes he has seen in the neighborhood has been the arrival of Latinos and Asians.

■ We cross Vienna and continue upward toward Athens. Above the garage at No. 520 is a decorative row of pine cones and false miniature pine trees and a stabile that moves with the wind current. We now see the landscape behind us in a wide-angled view.

■ At Athens we ascend Peru Stwy. This hillside was a dumping ground and an eyesore until a grass roots group, Hilltop Block Club, banded together. After five years of dedicated work, they were able, in cooperation with the Recreation and Park Department and the Open Space committee, to retain Richard Schadt, landscape architect, to design the hillside garden and stairway. Seventy neighborhood residents cooperated in digging, planting and watering more than 150 trees and shrubs, raised by the nursery at Golden Gate Park. The basic work was completed in 1982.

■ The serpentine stairway is built of aggregate and railroad ties; the walkway is aggregate, which adds a touch of luxury. (City-planned walkways and stairways are usually concrete.) The trees that have done well on the slopes are Australian willows, myoperum, Italian pine, flowering plums. The rock roses look healthy, and the acacia trees are in bloom. The light of this overcast day has accented areas of shrubbery I had not noticed before. The view is breathtaking.

■ At the top, on Valmar Ter., we enter an open grassy knoll, (a perfect place to sit and read or look), that the neighbor on the left cares for. She waters, picks up garbage, and plants flowers on her adjoining lot so that everyone can enjoy the green space.

■ We continue on Peru. No. 715 is a three-bedroom cottage (circa 1907) on a lot below the street level. (The view at this point takes in San Francisco General Hospital, the shipyards, Mt. Diablo across the Bay, and to the left of that, Roundtop Peak.) No. 747 is also below street level. Above the number is a little Buddha, and on the charming front patio other religious icons are displayed. Lemon trees are growing in the yard and a penthouse had been built facing the east. A pittosporum enhances the front gate. To the right is the blue water tower in McLaren Park.

Excelsior

No. 837 is the checkerboard, multicolored garage attached to a small frame house. The brown stucco hood above the entrance gives it a Hansel-and-Gretel look.

■ At the crossroads of Peru and Burrows, the macadam road and the adjoining park make us feel as though we are out for a country walk. We take the path that might be the continuation of Peru into McLaren Park. After we enter the park, take the footpath to the right. A red-tailed hawk is on the power line, and now he's flying into the Monterey cypress. We pass by a basketball court, sand box, picnic tables, benches, a trash can—all conveniently set out for people to enjoy the park.

■ John McLaren Park is 317.97 acres. In 1905, Daniel Burnham, the city planner from Chicago, suggested the land be used as a park. In 1929, the Board of Supervisors proposed a park to be named after John McLaren, who was supervisor of Golden Gate Park for 60 years, and in 1977, 72 years later, the land was bought for 3.5 million dollars.

■ At the first crossroads, where there is a refuse container, take the left path. Ahead of us to the right we see the radio towers on Mt. San Bruno. We take the route to our right heading toward the water tower. To our left we see the Southern hills. The view in front of us and to our sides makes me wish for 500-degree, wide-angled eyes. We have gone around the water tower; next to a ceonothus bush is a descending footpath. At the first fork in the road, we take the footpath to our right, pass the 13-step stairway to Prague, and walk down the Excelsior Stwy. to Munich.

■ Turn right and walk up the Ina Stwy. that begins at Excelsior. As we ascend and look to the left, we see the Public Health Hospital. Toward the center we see the playing field of City College. At the top of the stairs we're encircled by a view. We're in the La Grande Ave. cul-de-sac.

■ No. 73 Mansfield is a charming little house surrounded by trees. We turn left on La Grande to Avalon. (The #54 bus stops here.) Turn left on Avalon and ascend the Athens Stwy. to our right.

■ The hillside is overgrown with broom. As we go up, a panoramic view from the left comes into focus. A nice walkway, with ivy and a Monterey pine is at the top. Ahead of us are views to the east.

■ No. 246 Athens was built in 1907; No. 242, in 1912. No. 90 Athens (circa 1924) is one of my favorite tuck-ins because I imagine how I would like to fix it up: it's a frame house with a veranda and pitched roof, set in a large lot that any gardener would envy. At the top of this hill we are approximately 350 feet high, and we are gingerly walking downhill. The driveway at No. 46 is very steep, and it's easy to imagine No. 44 with a moat.

■ Turn left on Vienna. City College comes into view when we look back. (Trees are missing on this street.) Note the angular design on No. 70. It almost looks like a Native American motif. On the left side of the house is a half-barrel planter; the long-stemmed flower is painted on the wall.

Cross Peru and continue on Vienna. No. 274 has a noteworthy descending driveway. In the middle of the intersection of Vienna and Excelsior is the roundabout used for traffic control.

Right turn on Excelsior (600 block). The houses in this block were built during a 1927 carpenters' strike. Production had halted on the Laguna and Pacific apartments, so the carpenters came to this area. The Mission Bottling Plant, which was at the corner, bottled spring water and manufactured soft drinks.

No. 536 Excelsior has a totem pole depicting various heads of animals and people; No. 513 was built in 1904.

From a glance, we see a very good group of row Queen Annes on the 200 block of Edinburgh, but they need painting.

We're on the 400 block of Excelsior. The Monroe Elementary School is at the corner at No. 260 Madrid. On both sides of Madrid are row Queen Annes.

I like Nos. 336, 318, 310, 308. To our left on Lisbon, we find another good selection of row Queen Annes.

We're at Excelsior and Paris. The San Francisco Community Alternate School, formerly known as Excelsior School, is at the corner. The bakery near the corner of Mission, the Panaderia, is now closed. The mural on the bakery wall was dedicated to the people of Outer Mission by the Excelsior youth club. It features an illustrated map of the district, and people waiting for the #52 bus.

We cross Mission. No. 4434 was formerly the Batters Box with electrically-powered batting cages for hardball and softball. Walk to our left and turn right at Santa Rosa to see Corpus Christi Church at No. 62. In 1921, it became a regular territorial parish to better serve the heterogeneous population that was moving toward the Excelsior neighborhood. No. 69 dates back to 1906. We can get a good look at Alemany Blvd., the old Oceanshore railroad bed.

Return to Mission and walk over to your right to get a feeling of the old shopping neighborhood on this block of the street. The apartments above No. 4540 have their own artesian wells, but are required to use City water. No. 4555 Mission, the Excelsior Fish & Poultry has been here 50 years. It carries an excellent supply of fish, including whole fish, and buffalo and carp from Louisiana. There are many open-air produce markets on the street, plus restaurants like Joe's Fish Grotto, at No. 4435, and, further up toward Silver, the Cable Car Joe's Restaurant at No. 4320, where we can see the chuck steak being ground. We walk to Mission and Cotter to our beginning.

Walk 23

GLEN CANYON PARK
& GLEN CANYON
Twittons and Canyons

After Mexico became independent of Spain in 1821, settlement and private ownership of California lands was encouraged by large grants awarded to high-ranking officials. In 1845, Rancho San Miguel, which included present-day Glen Park, was given to Jose Noe, the last alcade, or mayor, under Mexican rule.

After the Mexican War of 1846, Noe became a United States government official. Although his land holdings were guaranteed, he lost them in various disputes. Eventually, they were sold to developers and homestead associations.

Three people who bought large sections of Rancho San Miguel played important roles in the San Francisco community: Francois Pioche, a Frenchman who later established the famous Poodle Dog Restaurant, a San Francisco landmark for more than a century; Adolph Sutro, from Bavaria, who left a legacy of planted areas and parks in the western part of the city (Mt. Sutro was part of the Rancho); and Behrend Joost, a German, who, in 1891, built the electric streetcars that connected Glen Park to the rest of San Francisco.

Glen Park became the dairy area in the 1850s, after Cow Hollow was condemned due to a cholera outbreak.

The Crocker Estate Company eventually gained control of Glen Park. Describing it as "a veritable Switzerland", their ads in a 1908 newspaper

MAP 23

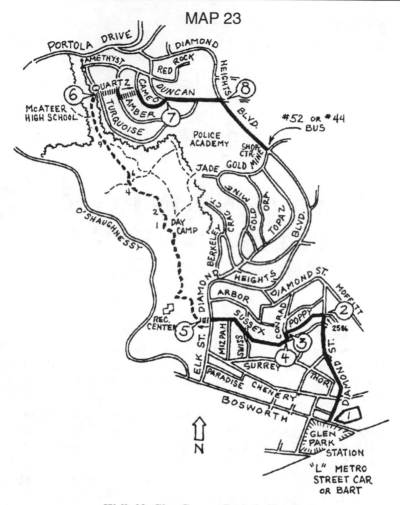

Walk 23: Glen Canyon Park & Glen Park

Public Transportation: J Church Metro that comes into the Bart Station at Bosworth and Diamond is an excellent way to allow us to manuever in several possible directions and still find accessible transportation close at hand.

1. Begin at Bosworth and Diamond. North on Diamond to No. 2586.
2. Left on Poppy Lane to Conrad.
3. Left on Conrad.
4. Right on Sussex. Cross Diamond Heights Blvd, descend stairway into Glen Canyon.
5. Take footpath into Canyon. Walk on nature trail along Islais Creek to Quartz.
6. Exit on footpath that leads to stairway to Turquoise (next to No. 48) and then to Amber (next to No. 166). Right on Amber to No. 289. Walk up stairway to Cameo.
7. Right on Duncan.
8. Right on Diamond Heights Blvd. to Gold Mine for bus #52 to Bosworth or bus #44.

exhorted people eager to make money, to buy improved lots that cost $300 to $500 each, and to pay them off at the rate of $5 per month.

Glen Canyon Park was bought by San Francisco in 1922, and the surrounding area was sold for homesites.

■ We begin our walk at the Glen Park Station at Bosworth and Diamond. Walking north on Diamond (for food, turn right on Chenery), to No. 2586, we turn left into Poppy Lane, a homey access alley, or as the British call it, a twitton. During blackberry season we wear long sleeves and bring small containers.

■ We turn left on Conrad and right on Sussex. Cross Diamond Heights Blvd. to the entrance of Glen Canyon. Descend the stairway to follow the nature trail. CAUTION: STAY ON THE TRAIL TO MINIMIZE THE DANGER OF TOUCHING POISON OAK. BE AWARE!!! DO NOT PICK FLOWERS, OR DISTURB NESTS OR HABITAT. DO NOT LITTER.

■ The accompanying map and self-guided tour of Glen Canyon comes from the Recreation and Park Department of the City. They have designated a trail that illustrates some of the habitats in the canyon. We have included a few of the numbers on the map to highlight some important areas. While walking you may see many birds in the canyon. You will probably see the red-tailed hawks and the American kestrels flying overhead looking for rodents.

■ No. 2: this part of the grasslands is a riot of colors during spring wildflower time. There are poppies and lupine and Douglas Iris and mustard. No. 4: this small hollow depends upon the springs coming out from here for water. Many mourning doves come here to quench their thirst. Sparrows and towhees and house finches also like this area. No. 6: Islais Creek that runs through Glen Canyon (this is the last of it that runs above ground), is one of three running creeks in San Francisco. Plants that love water are here—willows and sedges and horsetails. No. 9: This is the beginning and end of the canyon. About a hundred yards away, the spring waters flow from under Twin Peaks.

■ We continue on the trail to Turquoise (unmarked). Cross Turquoise, then take the stairway to Amber. Right turn on Amber to #289. Ascend stairway to Cameo. Follow Cameo around to the right. Right on Duncan, then right on Diamond Heights Blvd. to Gold Mine and the bus.

■ From old Glen Park where we see small homes and row Queen Annes and feel a settled-in snugness, to Diamond Heights, relatively new, and more diffident, is a canyon away. It's not too difficult to imagine the hills without the houses, and Islais Creek running full. (One Glen Park dweller related some of his childhood activities to me: catching frogs in Islais Creek, hunting rabbits in the hills, and even hiding out in a cave on Red

Poppy Lane

Rock Hill for a week after running away from home at age thirteen.) Because neighborhood activists are alert to any potential building activity that would alter the ecological balance of Glen Canyon, we residents of the City have been able to enjoy an unusual natural canyon almost in the middle of San Francisco.

Walk 24

DIAMOND HEIGHTS & UPPER NOE VALLEY
Rocks, Minerals and H₂O

Diamond Heights neighborhood was built on 325 acres of craggy, hilly terrain, after World War II, when federal redevelopment money became available for construction. A variety of modest-to-luxurious homes, townhouses, apartments, and condominiums, were built, trees were planted, and stairways were constructed. Diamond Heights is bounded by important corridor streets, O'Shaughnessy Blvd., Portola Dr., Clipper St., and Diamond Heights Blvd.; and by a 300-foot-deep Glen Canyon that separates it from Miraloma to the west, and Glen Park to the east.

■ We begin at the shopping center corner of Diamond Heights Blvd., No. 5290, and Gold Mine Dr.,to walk south on Diamond Heights Blvd. At the crossroads, turn left on Diamond St. and and follow the curve to Beacon St. I love to take visitors here to expose them to the remarkable vista as we promenade along the ridge of Beacon, on the new footpath. The hillside is part of the Open Space program, but people love shortcuts, and we see cycle tracks and walking tracks down the slope.

■ The Harry Stwy. begins between Nos. 190 and 200 Beacon. It is surrounded by tall trees and almost hidden behind high vegetation; and the air is redolent with pine. There is a country atmosphere about this stairway.

■ The long and rather steep Harry Stwy., constructed from various materials—wood, concrete and cobblestone—is one of the most delightful in the City. The variety of homes alongside, with their decks and wide windows, establish an individual style to the vicinity. Near the top of the stairway, Yerba Buena Island to the east and the spires of St. Paul's Cathedral toward the north are clearly visible. As we descend, the Bay Bridge and downtown San Francisco emerge, while immediately around us the African daisies, ivy, geraniums, fuchsia, wild onion, pittisporum, yucca, lily of the Nile and pyracantha provide a celebration of color.

■ The Harry Stwy. ends at Laidley, where we turn right. New and remodeled contemporary-style dwellings have recently been built here.— like No. 102 by Jeremy Kotas, and Nos. 128 and 136—which provide visual interest and a foil for the traditional small homes on the street.

■ The palatial 3-story, Second Empire and Italianate home, No. 192– 194, near Fairmount, now an apartment house, was built by attorney Cecil Poole in 1872, and bought by Thomas Bell, a San Francisco financier, and his wife Teresa, protege of Mary Ann Pleasant (commonly known as Mammy Pleasant). There seems to be evidence, more or less, that Pleasant, a black woman who was born a free person in Philadelphia, was a mystery figure, a dedicated Abolitionist, a cook working for wealthy families, owner of laundries, boarding houses and a brothel, controlled Bell and his wife, and may have assisted in his fatal fall down the stairs.

■ Turn left on Fairmount. No. 226 is a tuck-in where the residents enjoy an enviable view. We make a right turn on Whitney, a small street with several row Queen Annes. No. 223, an eclectic, is newly-renovated. Turn right on Chenery (the main shopping street of Glen Park). It has a coffee house, bakery, hardware store and the branch library. At Miguel, turn right and walk uphill to Bemis; turn left to Amatista Stwy. to ascend to Everson. A shopping center was proposed for the triangle near the top of the stairs, but residents opposed it, and the area is now a small park.

■ Everson is one of the oldest sections of the Diamond Heights Redevelopment Area. We learn from a resident that her home and the house at No. 50 Everson, which was made with lumber from the 1939 Golden Gate International Exposition on Treasure Island, were the only two structures on the street in 1957.

■ Turn right on Digby St., where we pass larger homes (watch the signs carefully here), or continue on Everson for a better view. Pass Everson, Addison, the fire-station. We are on Addison as we walk alongside the delightful Walter Haas Playground, an inviting place for picnicking, playing and just sitting.

■ Continue to Diamond Heights Blvd., cross the street, turn left. At Berkeley Way, we turn right. Next to No. 99, walk down Onique Stwy. to the lower loop of Berkeley Way that adjoins Glen Canyon Park.

■ Carnivals, parades, picnics, dances, and other amusements took place in Glen Canyon Park in the 1800s. The canary-trainer from the Cliff House often ascended in a gas-filled balloon, or walked a tightrope across the canyon on Sundays. Bears, monkeys and elephants were special features of the small zoo. Around 1907, the Crocker Estates Company put in private tennis and basketball courts to rent to organizations. Local residents, aggrieved at having their children play out on the streets, lobbied the city to purchase the land. In 1922, the Board of Supervisors made the first payment on the 104 acres in Glen Canyon Park.

■ Continue to see the extraordinary rock formation near the corner of Crags Ct. A resident who was one of the first to buy on Crags Ct. did so because he wanted to practice rock climbing.

MAP 24

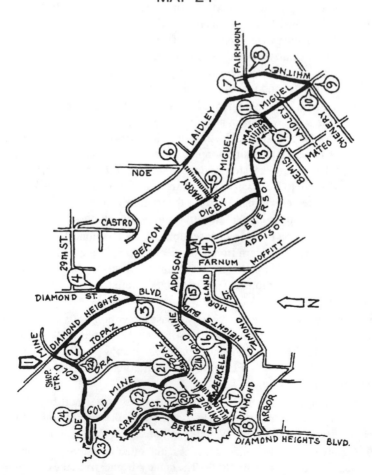

■ Continue around Crags Ct. into Berkeley Way. There are lots of eucalyptus in this area. Next to No. 100, ascend Onique Stwy. At the top we are next to No. 400 Gold Mine. Cross the street, and at the top we are next to No. 243 Topaz.

■ Turn left on Topaz, right on Gold Mine Dr. (679 feet above sea level). Walk left into Jade Pl. for a panoramic view of the Bay Bridge and skyscrapers. Continue around to your left, walking downhill on Gold Mine Dr. to our beginning.

■ An alternate route that I like very much is to turn right on Topaz. As we walk along the ridge nearing No. 131, an extraordinary sight spreads out in front of us—a view to the east and south. Continue down the hill to Gold Mine, bearing right to our beginning.

WALK 24: Diamond Heights Route

Public Transportation: Muni #52 stops at Diamond Heights Blvd. and Gold Mine.

1. Begin at Diamond Heights Blvd. shopping center No. 5290 and Gold Mine Dr.
2. Walk south on Diamond Heights Blvd. to Diamond St.
3. Left on Diamond St. to Beacon.
4. Right on Beacon to Harry Stwy. next to No.190 Beacon.
5. Descend stairway to Laidley.
6. Right on Laidley.
7. Left on Fairmount.
8. Right on Whitney.
9. Right on Chenery.
10. Right on Miguel.
11. Left on Bemis.
12. Right to Amatista Stwy. Ascend.
13. Continue to Digby and bear right.
14. Continue straight ahead on Addison to Diamond Heights Blvd.
15. Cross the Blvd. Left on Diamond Heights Blvd. to Berkeley Way.
16. Right on Berkeley Way.
17. Next to No. 99, left to descend Onique Stwy.
18. Right on Berkeley Way to see rock formation near corner of Crags Ct.
19. Go to end of Crags Ct. Return and continue across on Berkeley Way.
20. Next to No. 100 Berkeley Way, ascend stairway to Gold Mine (No. 400). Continue up Onique Stwy. to Topaz (No. 243).
21. Left on Topaz.
22. Right on Gold Mine Dr.
23. Walk into Jade Pl. for view.
24. Continue on Gold Mine to our beginning.

Alternate route from No. 21:
21A. Right on Topaz.
22A. Right on Gold Mine Dr. to our beginning.

Harry Street

Walk 25

MT. DAVIDSON
Now You See It, Now You Don't

Generically, Mt. Davidson is part of the enormous area west of Twin
Peaks. Specifically, it surrounds Mt. Davidson, (at 927 feet, the highest
hill in San Francisco), and in itself is an interesting mixture of sub-
neighborhood sections. We traverse several: Sherwood Forest (there's a
Robin Hood Dr. here), Westwood Highlands, and Mt. Davidson/Miraloma
Park. From the larger homes toward the west and north of Mt. Davidson, to
the smaller ones in the eastern Miraloma sections, our walk is a field trip
in applied sociology, vis-a-vis real estate and architecture.

■ We begin at the junction of Juanita Alley and Miraloma Dr. To the left
of us on Miraloma, new street trees, Prunus cellulata have been planted
by the Friends of the Urban Forest. Turn right on Miraloma, walking uphill
on the left-hand side, a street with many trees, views, large unattached
homes and long, wide alleyways. Walking on the even-numbered side, we
can feel the elevation, we can look down on the West Portal neighborhood,
and we can see the buildings of the Christian Science Retreat on Ulloa.
■ Next to No. 95 is the narrow Bengal Stwy., that we ascend, a dirt path
strewn with eucalyptus leaves; and stairs of cobblestone and concrete,
with wooden risers. It's a lovely feeling to ascend the stairway on a city
street, walk through a eucalyptus forest, and come out at the top on a very
sunny city street, Lansdale. Across from us is a whitewashed brick
structure with Spanish tiles surrounding the doorway, and heavy wooden
shutters on the sides of the windows.
■ Turn right on Lansdale; then right on Casitas. No. 265 is a baronial
home high above a retaining wall and higher still on additional flagstone

stilts. The house continues around the corner, paralleling our route, as the new addition, the redwood tree house and the flagstone chimney, come into sight. The view to the north encompasses the heights of Forest Hill, Edgehill, and to the south, the San Bruno Mountains with homes terraced in figure-eight patterns.

■ Turn left on Cresta Vista, which was formerly a cul-de-sac. The houses date to 1949, after which the street was extended. One of the residents who loves living on Cresta Vista says his views are to the south, (on a clear day they can see San Jose), the east and the west, including the ocean. Except for the rainy months, and the foggy months during the summer, the days sparkle.

■ Next to No. 96, we walk down Globe Alley Stwy., a combination easement and stairway. There is ample room along the side for flowers

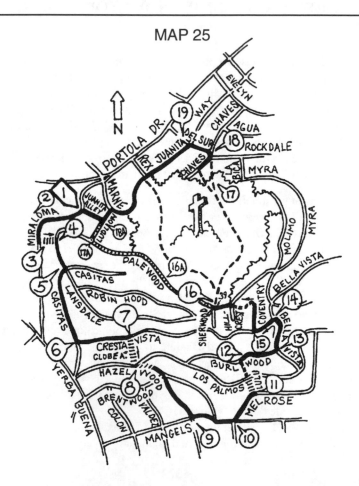

MAP 25

and shrubs. At the bottom of the stairway we are at the juncture of Los Palmos (the end) and Hazelwood Ave. We cross the street, descend eight steps and walk left and downward on Hazelwood. The sign says Hazelwood 425 to the right. We go to our left. Walk on the odd-numbered side for the views. We are on the 400 block. Near the juncture of Hazelwood and Greenwood we see the radio towers perched on Mt. San Bruno.

■ Continue on Hazelwood (300 block). The homes are detached, mostly built of stucco; tile roofs are common, the streets are wide and well kept, the air is fresh, and every structure seems to gleam.

■ At the corner of Hazelwood and Mangels, we turn left on Mangels. The aroma of rosemary growing over the length of the low wall on the corner of Brentwood is pleasing. The houses on our left are on a higher elevation.

WALK 25: Mt. Davidson Route

Public Transportation: Muni #43 bus stops at Miraloma Dr. and Juanita.

1. Begin at Juanita Alley and Miraloma Dr.
2. Right on Miraloma.
3. Next to No. 95, ascend Bengal Stairway plus dirt path and cobble Stwy. Caution—watch footing.
4. Right on Lansdale.
5. Right on Casitas.
6. Left on Cresta Vista.
7. Next to #98 descend Globe Alley walkway/Stwy. to junction of Los Palmos and Hazelwood Ave. Cross Los Palmos.
8. Descend eight steps. Walk left and downward on Hazelwood.
9. Left on Mangels.
10. Left on Melrose.
11. Between Nos. 480 and 500, ascend Lulu Alley. Cross Los Palmos to continue on Lulu footpath. (When muddy, walk on Los Palmos to Bella Vista.)
12. Right on Burlwood.
13. Left on Bella Vista.
14. Left on Cresta Vista Dr.
15. Right on Coventry. Go left on Myra. Bear right to Dalewood.
16. Take path into Park across from #39 Dalewood Way. Path is narrow. Do not take the first right hand path. Take the second right turn path downward. It is wide. Continue to La Bica and Rockdale. During muddy conditions, skip to 16A.
17. Left on Rockdale, Right on Chavez.
18. Left on Del Sur.
19. Left to Juanita Way, past Rex, past Marne. Right on Juanita Alley to Miraloma and to our beginning.

16A. If you don't wish to walk through the park, continue on Dalewood Way to Ludlow.
17A. Right on Ludlow to Juanita.
18A. Left on Juanita Alley to Miraloma to our beginning.

At the corner of Mangels and Melrose, we bear left on Melrose. The houses here are attached and noticeably smaller. Between Nos. 500 and 480 Melrose ascend Lulu Alley Stwy. Ascend. The woodsy setting is lovely, but I think more work can be done to make the sides along the stairway attractive. The red cotoneaster berries provide a focal point among the pines. We come to Los Palmos. To our right are new homes, in pastel colors, beautifully sited.

We cross Los Palmos to continue up the Lulu Stwy., which is now a steep footpath among the eucalyptus. I think stairs here would help prevent erosion. (When it's muddy, walk on Los Palmos to Bella Vista.) Continue to Burlwood. Across the street is a high slope. We are getting closer to the south side of Mt. Davidson.

Turn right on Burlwood and then left on Bella Vista Way, but not before looking to our right and seeing the blue water tower in McLaren Park and the hills to the south. The corner of Bella Vista Way that abuts the slope would benefit from community garden work. Ahead of us we see the top of Mt. Davidson.

Turn left on Cresta Vista. Spanish words like "cresta" (hillside) and "vista" (view) can only lead us upward.

Turn right on Coventry, and again upward. Between Nos. 89 and 95 is a hidden walkway called Coventry Lane. Again we are transported psychologically out of the city as we walk the grooved cement lane, find the ivy entwined around the wood slats of the fences and houses built among the eucalyptus.

We arrive at a conjunction of circular streets—Hillcrest, Myra, Sherwood. There is another sign saying, Lansdale End and Dalewood 000. Follow Dalewood Way and take the path across from No. 39 into the park. A white metal barrier across the path restricts it to pedestrian use only.

We bear toward the downward path so that we come out near our starting point. At the first fork in the road, we take the lower one. Again, at the next fork, we take the one to the right, down hill. This is the perfect place for a stairway, I think. At the third fork in the road, we go to our left, then to our right, downhill. At the next fork there is a stairway made of logs to our right. We take it and arrive between Nos. 925 and 919 Rockdale. (It is also possible to take the path to the left.) The houses here are unattached but small.

We turn left on Rockdale. At the crossroad of Rockdale 900 and Chavez End, we walk right on Chavez to Del Sur. Walk six steps down on Del Sur to Juanita. Turn left. Look at No. 226. It is an amalgam of several devices that I think are humorous—a columnar entrance topped by a dunce cap on the right; and on the left, a miniature repetition of this pattern, with the narrowest window I've seen.

■ Continuing on Juanita, cross Rex. On our left, we see in close-up the Franciscan Formation that composes Mt. Davidson. To our right, across Portola Dr., we see a house (octagonal, I think) on a cliff in the Edgehill neighborhood. We bear left to Dalewood Way, which skirts Mt. Davidson. At the bottom of the hill, we bear right on Lansdale, where we may see a hydrangea bush at No. 4 with 21-inch flowers! What better testimonial to fog?

■ We turn left on Juanita to Miraloma, to our starting point.

■ Just for fun, go one block farther northeast to Marne Ave. to see an extraordinary sight: the Mt. Davidson Cross, above a convex-shaped border of Monterey pine and cypress seems to shift like the moon as we walk. Now you see it—now you don't.

■ If you want to arrive at the starting point without going through the park, follow Dalewood Way, bear right on Lansdale, turn left on Juanita to Miraloma.

Walk 26

MIRALOMA PARK
The Walk of Left-Sided Views

The Miraloma Park walk skirts around the eastern side of Mt. Davidson, known in the 1850s as Blue Mountain. In 1911, the mountain was renamed in honor of George Davidson (1825–1911), who first surveyed the mountain. He was recognized internationally as a brillliant scientist, became president of the California Academy of Sciences and made San Francisco his permanent home for 61 years.

Although it is the highest hill in San Francisco, it is so thickly covered with eucalyptus and pine trees, (planted by Adolph Sutro in the 1880s), that it does not afford a view, except toward the southeast from the chaparral side. However, some of the most inspiring views in the entire city may be seen from streets like Marietta Dr. and Bella Vista, without the 20-minute wait that is often obligatory from the top of Telegraph Hill.

■ We begin at the intersection of Juanita Way and Marne, walking on Juanita toward the 200 block. We pass several *Prunus cellulata* street trees that have been planted by the Friends of the Urban Forest in cooperation with Juanita Way neighbors, and farther along an inviting stone stairway next to No. 270. We marvel at the dynamic patterns of the striated, veined chert as we walk alongside the hill.

■ Stucco has been the material of choice for the homes along the street. The small bungalow sizes, the variety of rooflines and styles, from Normandy to half-timbered, all contribute to a surprising look for San Francisco. We have the impression this is an escaped Los Angeles neighborhood.

■ We continue to the corner of Evelyn, where, when we look back, we see the Mt. Davidson Cross in profile; we continue to see it as we turn right on Evelyn, and then right again on Teresita Blvd; passing Chavez, we still have it in our purview. The colors of the houses are mostly white to off-white, lending to everything a fresh, bright look. Strolling past the water reservoir at Agua, we are exposed to new vistas emerging on our left.

■ Continuing on Teresita, we pass Isola, and walk on the odd-numbered side to scan the views between the houses. From the corner of Reposa, we see part of the Diamond Heights neighborhood toward the left.

■ The Miraloma Community Church is farther on at Arroyo, where we turn left toward Marietta. A profuse stand of red-hot-poker belongs to No. 199. Turn right on Marietta Dr. to walk on the upper sidewalk where the attached houses follow the slope. Eucalyptus trees and cotoneaster bushes and bottlebrush demark the lower and upper sections of the street. Around No. 376 we look to the left to obtain a superior view of Glen Park Canyon, which divides Diamond Heights from Miraloma Park. At No. 380 an expanding landscape dotted with church steeples and radio towers and rocky canyons unfolds as we look toward the south and east.

■ We're glad to have binoculars along because we see an extraordinary sight from No. 396 Marietta: the rock formation in the foreground; the crane at the Hunters Point Naval Shipyard; Bayview; McLaren Park with its blue water tower; Candlestick Park; the crisscross pattern of houses in the southern hills, and San Bruno Mountains!

■ We curve around to our right and follow upper Marietta where the houses date from the 1950s and 1960s. From the corner of Teresita, follow the street to our left, then cross the Teresita crosswalk, to walk to Molimo.

■ Turn right on Molimo 000 and walk on the odd-numbered side. Next to No. 95 is Gatun Alley, a concrete easement. Turn left, and walk down to Foerster. Near the bottom is a terminal box belonging to Pacific Bell.

■ Turn right on Foerster, walking downhill, and right again on Los Palmos. The house at the corner, No. 795 Foerster, has a cactus garden in the front yard, and a more extensive one in the backyard. Passing Stanford Heights, we continue uphill on Los Palmos.

■ We turn right on Bella Vista. From the top of the hill at Bella Vista and Burlwood, we look backward to see a breathtaking panorama. Walk across the street from the odd-numbered to the even-numbered side, looking at the view continually until the vista to the north opens up and we see the Bay and the Outer Mission. The cluster of brick buildings is the Jewish Home for the Aged on Silver Ave.

■ Bear right on Bella Vista Way—the name is inscribed in the pavement. The corner of Bella Vista and Molimo is an outstanding viewing station for White-crowned sparrows. Nearby is an undeveloped site slated for a proposed 9-home development.

■ Continue on Bella Vista to the 200 block for a spectacular scene. We can pinpoint the water tower in McLaren Park, the buildings in Glen Park neighborhood and in Outer Mission. Walk up the stairway next to No. 222. The plants along the sides have been nurtured by a neighbor.

■ At the top is Myra Way. We can end the walk here and hop on a #36 bus—but a superspectacular view is in store for us farther on.

■ Turn left on Myra Way, looking to our left at the continuous views. At the corner of Myra 500 and Molimo 400, we turn right on Molimo, which becomes a cul-de-sac. Next to No. 513 Molimo Dr. is a railroad-tie stairway and a footpath to Mt. Davidson, which we ascend. Chaparral is dominant on this side of the hill.

MAP 26

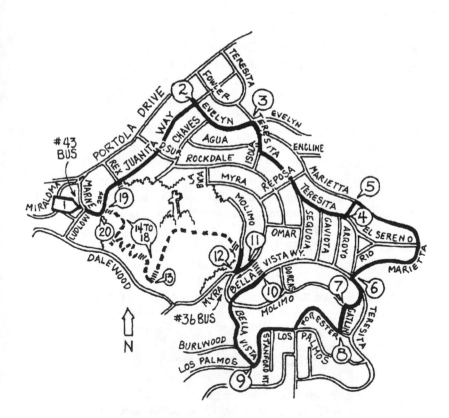

■ As we go upward, we can pivot around to view the circumference of San Francisco!

■ Downtown San Francisco comes into view, and of course the Sutro tower seems very close to us. At O'Shaughnessy, off Portola Dr., we see a ring of houses behind the shopping center. We follow the path on our right, but by reversing our point of view, we can pinpoint some buildings at middle distance: St. John's School on Chenery, a beige building with a bell tower; Simpson Bible College on Silver Ave., a red brick structure with a symmetrical row of windows; and the Jewish Home for the Aged, also of red brick.

■ Southbound traffic on Highway 280, the freeway nearest us, is hidden from view by the Glen Park BART station on Bosworth St. Below, O'Shaughnessy Blvd. outlines the contours of the Miraloma neighborhood and separates it from Glen Canyon Park and Diamond Heights.

WALK 26: Miraloma Park Route

Public Transportation: Muni #43 Masonic stops at Juanita and Marne.

1. Begin at Juanita and Marne. Walk on Juanita toward the 200 block.
2. Right on Evelyn to Teresita.
3. Right on Teresita past Isola and Reposa to Arroyo.
4. Left on Arroyo.
5. Right on Marietta Dr. Walk on upper Marietta. Curve to right and follow street. At the corner of Teresita, cross street to our left, then cross Teresita crosswalk.
6. Right on Molimo Dr. 000.
7. Next to No. 95, walk down Gatun Alley to Foerster.
8. Right on Foerster. Right on Los Palmos. Pass Stanford Heights.
9. Right on Bella Vista. Bear right on Bella Vista Wy.(great view at corner of Bella Vista and Molimo). Continue to 200 block for view.
10. Ascend stairway next to No. 222 Bella Vista to Myra Way. One can end the walk here, and hop on the #36, or continue.
11. Left on Myra Wy.
12. Right on Molimo at the corner of Myra 500 and Molimo 400. Next to No. 513, walk up stairway and follow footpath to the right on Mt. Davidson. Go toward the platform, turn left to descend the stone stairs to trail.
13. Right on footpath to another set of stairs.
14. Descend, cross dirt road. Continue down main trail.
15. At fork, bear right, downward on main trail.
16. At next fork, bear left around hill.
17. Bear right, downward. (Left fork goes to Dalewood.)
18. Bear left at antiquated fountain.
19. Descend stone stairway next to No. 275 Juanita.
20. Left to our beginning.

■ Underneath the platform on which the 1934 Cross stands, is a crypt containing religious relics. We turn to the left of the Cross to descend the stone stairway which will take us on a delightful interlude through the eucalyptus forest. Turn right on the footpath, go past the two sawed-off tree stumps, one shaped into a seat, and continue to another set of stone stairs. Descend and cross the dirt road to walk down the main trail.

■ At the fork in the road, bear right on the main trail. At the next fork, bear left around the hill. Bear right, downward. (The left fork goes to Dalewood.) Bear left at what looks like a disfunctional, stone drinking fountain.

■ We end the walk by descending the beautifully-cut stone stairway next to No. 284 Juanita. Walk left to our beginning.

Walk 27

CROSS-CITY WALK
Through an Up and Down City

Mike Hayman developed a 12-mile Cross-City stairway walk that begins at the Castro Muni station at Castro and 17th Sts. and ends at the Ferry Building, at Market and Embarcadero. It is an excellent way to see how the stairways provide pedestrian corridors throughout the City.

Since it is impossible to indicate all the turns, we suggest you carry a good city map; the numbered squares on the accompanying map designate areas where we have detailed neighborhood walks. Bring a lunch and oranges to sustain you.

WALK 27: Cross-City Route

Public Transportation: Muni Bus #8, #24, #37 Corbett, Metro Lines L, M, K stop at Castro and 17th Sts.

1. Begin at Castro Muni Station at Castro and 17th St.
2. North to Beaver Stwy. to Corona Heights Park, to Roosevelt Way to Levant; down Vulcan Stwy., up Saturn Stwy. to Roosevelt to Clifford to Upper Ter.; up stairway on right to Mt. Olympus.
3. Descend stairway to 17th St., to Clayton; south, up Pemberton Stwy. to Crown Ter.: north to Clarendon to Footbridge; right to Ashwood to Blairwood Stwy. to Crestmont.
4. Down Oakhurst Stwy. to Warren. Right to Lawton to 8th Ave.
5. South to Linares to Ventura; 2nd stairway on right to Sotelo to Lopez to Castenada to stairway on right to Mendoza.
6. 10th to Pacheco to Oriole Stwy. to Mandalay Stwy. to 15th Ave. Proceed north.
7. Ortega Stwy. on right to 14th Ave; to Aerial Stwy. to Funston.
8. Down Cascade Stwy. to Ortega Way to 14th to Moraga Stwy. to Grand View Park to new Moraga Stwy. to Lomita Stwy. to Kirkham. Left on 9th Ave. to Lincoln Way to Strybing Aboretum in Golden Gate Park for lunch stop and restrooms.
9. East to Stow Lake area to walk up and down Huntington Stwy. to Strawberry Hill.

147

MAP 27

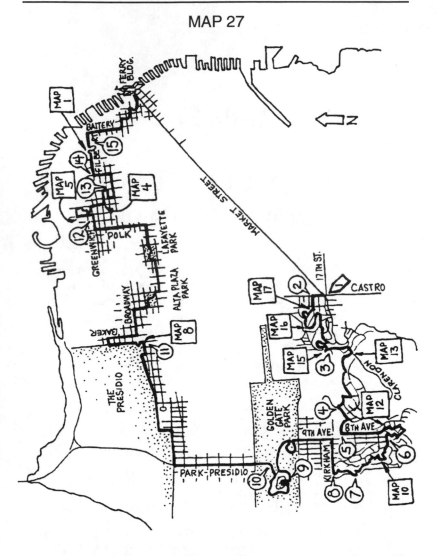

10. To Rose Garden to Park Presidio, north to Mountain Lake Park, east along Presidio Boundary.
11. Down Lyon Stwy. to Greenwich to Baker Stwy. to Broadway. East to Scott, right to Alta Plaza Park. East to Lafayette Park, east to Polk St. North to Greenwich Stwy. up to Hyde.
12. Turn left to Francisco; right to Leavenworth, right to Chestnut, up Montclair Stwy. Up Lombard, left on Hyde, down Greenwich to Leavenworth; Macondray Stwy. to Taylor.
13. Up Greenwich to Jones; down Vallejo Stwy. to Powell.
14. North to Filbert, east to Coit Tower on Telegraph Hill.
15. Down Filbert Stwy. to Levi's Plaza. Walk through to Battery, to Jackson, to Golden Gateway Center, to Embarcadero Center, to Ferry Bldg.

APPENDIX

List of Stairways

"Let's do it, it's only fair," I said to me.

But compiling a stairway list has been a difficult task. The parameters of the stairway are subject to question—there may be several corners, or no corner, or even no name for the stairway (like Pacheco Stwy). To sum it up: we had to practice good judgment. In every fairy tale, the completion of a very difficult task deserves a reward (perhaps a beautiful walking day).

Since this is an informal book, the ratings I have given the stairways are based purely on what struck me most during a walk: steepness, length, location, altitude, or beauty—and any combination in between.

No single factor can sum up the character of a stairway. It may be 100 steps, but easy (Diamond and 22nd St.) or 30 steps and difficult (Collingwood St.). There are charming stairways (Pemberton) or utilitarian stairways (Stonestown). We have elegant stairways (Alta Plaza Park) and we have rustic ones (Joy). We have stairways bordered by trees, shrubs, flowers, stones, broken glass, railings, Victorian houses, and lean-tos.

Stairways are difficult to push into categories—it seems easier to classify neighborhoods than stairways. Forest Hill and Forest Knolls are unusual in settings and stairways. Golden Gate Heights and Noe Valley have well-designed networks of stairways and retaining walls. Diamond Heights has series of very long stairways. Telegraph Hill and Russian Hill have alleys and stairways and many landlocked houses that have no access to a street. Living along Filbert and Greenwich stairways is an incentive to purchase lightweight everything—from furniture to groceries.

Russian Hill, surrounded by other hill neighborhoods, gives a feeling of greater separation with its cul-de-sacs within cul-de-sacs (Vallejo and Florence). Upper Market is an unusual conglomerate of leveled, fenced-off, or permanently closed-off stairways. The "unbuildable"empty lots in Bernal Heights and Twin Peaks have become sites for well-designed domiciles, East Bernal Heights is undergoing significant, dramatic changes, and will have a new look to it beginning in 1995. Pacific Heights is a wonderful contrast. The plan is controlled, the outlines orderly, the stairways purposefully designed.

The range of views in each neighborhood is exhilarating and subtle; the ambience indicative of what the neighborhood has to offer.

Above all, this is a participatory book. The fun is in the walking, in discovering your own variations, in the conversations struck up along the way, and in the marvelous views of an extraordinary City.

■ **Ratings.** Here is the rating system—strictly my own—that I used in rating the 330-plus stairways listed here. Feel free to disagree, vehemently, and we can set up an imaginary conversation between us, but I think my mind is made up.

No. 5   The Scheherazade category. These stairways surprise the walker, initially and forever after. They may be elegant or rustic, they may be short or long. But they exhibit variety, stir the imagination, and delight the senses. One can only love them madly, these Scheherazades.

No. 4   Impressive qualities with minor shortcomings and one outstanding aspect, or an extremely attractive section.

No. 3   Little known but deserves wider recognition because of the environs, man-made or natural. Neighborhood generally very attractive.

No. 2   Intrinsic to neighborhood history and ambience. Well-trodden. In most cases, the architectural context rates considerably higher than the stairway itself, or the view may be worth the visit. It's a pretty straightforward stairway of no great beauty.

No. 1   It may be so boring that you'll fall asleep on the first landing.

☆   A ☆ stair might be well worth visiting if it were located elsewhere—for example, in a safe neighborhood. This stairway is only for the knowledgeable resident, the wary aficionado.

/   The symbol / stands for the word "between."

■ **Anza Vista.** A neighborhood surrounding the University of San Francisco complex. Small well-kept homes from the 1950s and the Victorian era are part of this area.

2   Arbol Lane/Barcelona & Encanto & Turk. Next to No. 125 Anza Vista. *Good everyday route.*

2   Arguello/Anza & Edward into Rossi Recreation Center. *Large granite planter bowls at entrance of two granite stairways.*

2   Dicha Alley/Lupine & Wood. *Useful and used.*
2   Ewing/at Nos. 196-200, to Anza near Collins. *Ewing Court was a baseball field at one time. Clever.*
4   Lone Mountain/from 401 Parker to Beaumont and Stanyan. *Long twitton, trees, church spires, views of Angel Island and west; nice series of Victorians on McAllister off Parker.*

■ **Balboa Park.** Indian street names abound in this neighborhood. Also has underground waterways, a creek and the old Cayuga Lake.

2   Cayuga/Naglee & Alemany
2   Oneida/Alemany & Cayuga. *Practical.*
2   Rousseau/Alemany & Mission
■ **Bayview.** Some historic buildings in this neighborhood.

☆   Bayview Park. *All concrete.*
☆   Gilroy Street/Jamestown.
☆   Hawes & Innes.
☆   Innes (next to Mt. Spring).
☆   LaSalle/Mendall & Lane.
☆   Quesada/Newhall & 3rd Street.
☆   Thornton/3rd Street & Latona.

■ **Bernal Heights.** A neighborhood of blue-collar workers, artists and professionals. Many stairways/gardens under renovation.

2   Aztec/Shotwell & Stoneman. *Stoneman was a Union general in the Civil War.*
3   Brewster Stairway & Footpath/Rutledge, Costa & Mullen. *Next to No. 115 Rutledge. New, concrete. Flowers planted around stairway.*
2   Chapman & Bernal Heights Blvd. *Concrete. Native shrubs on slopes.*
2   Cortland/Prospect & Santa Marina. *Says, "Please walk on me."*
2   Coso Avenue/Prospect & Winfield. *View; cars from private driveway have to cross the stairs.*
3   Ellsworth and Bernal Heights Peak. *Leftover stone stairway. Refreshing view.*
4   Esmeralda/Winfield to Prospect to Lundys Lane to Coleridge.
3   Esmeralda/Brewster & Franconia. *Renovated. Elevated, timber and concrete; benches and lighting. Views.*
4   Eugenia/Prospect & Winfield. *Among trees.*
1   Eve Stairway/upper & lower Holladay/Wright & Peralta. *A wraith of itself.*

3 Fair Avenue/Coleridge & Prospect. *Rebuilt in more noble proportions. View.*

2 Faith Stairway/Bayshore & Holladay. *Part of a pedestrian overpass; an opportunity to hear increases in decibels from auto traffic.*

3 Faith/Brewster & Holladay. *New access.*

4 Franconia/Brewster & Franconia at Costa. *Community garden, 1991. Railroad tie stwy., trees, view toward Bay & Hunters Point.*

3 Franconia/Mullen & Montcalm. *Wooden, short. Shrubbery and trees alongside. View.*

2 Franconia/Mullen & Peralta. *Concrete.*

3 Harrison/Ripley & Norwich. *Wood and concrete stwy, benches, lighting. Great view of downtown. Builder/subdivider put in stwy. In transition.*

1 Holladay/Peralta & Adam.

4 Holladay/Peralta & Bayshore. *View. The link between an isolated, urban neighborhood and the main traffic arteries north and south.*

2 Holly Park/Bocana.

2 Holly Park/Highland.

2 Holly Park/Murray.

2 Holly Park/Park. *Across from muraled Junipero Serra School.*

5 Joy/Holladay & Brewster. *Rural. New wood stwy. and benches. Existing gardens to be preserved.*

3 Kingston/Coleridge & Prospect. *Semblance of floating stairs. Railing. Rock formation on side plus a long footpath.*

3 Mayflower/Holladay & Franconia. *New access, wood stwy., trees— maytens, oak, purple leaf plum.*

1 Mayflower/Bradford & Carver. *Railroad tie, short.*

5 Mirabel/at No. 11, to Precita. *Hidden. Extremely narrow.*

2 Montcalm/Wright & Peralta

3 Moultrie/Bernal Heights Blvd. & Powhattan. *Concrete plus footpath. Truly hidden and rural. Plantings alongside. First decisive victory of the Revolution was at Ft. Moultrie, S.C., in 1776.*

3 Mullen/Franconia. *Mullen is a fanciful land-locked 'street' in some spots. Enter at sign, "This is a nice neighborhood garden."*

2 Mullen, next to No. 146. *Concrete. Goes to next level.*

4 Nevada St. *Community Gardens.*

4 Peralta/Samoset & Mullen. *Magnificent gardens, extraordinary views.*

1 Richland/Mission & San Jose.

3 Rosenkranz/Chapman & Powhattan. *Rural, view, hillside plantings. Concrete with railing.*

4 Rutledge/Holladay, Mullen, Brewster, Peralta & Wolf Patch Community Garden. *Pedestrian path. Renovated; wide neighborhood use.*

3 Shotwell/Mirabel & Bessie. *Hidden; you wouldn't think to look for it. 1906 earthquake cottages on Shotwell. 12.5-foot-wide lots on Bessie.*
3 Tompkins/Putnam & Nevada. *Stairway in much better condition than nearby fence. New tree plantings. View of industrial side of the city.*
3 Virginia/Eugenia & Winfield. *Part of a stairway series from retaining wall to lower level.*

■ **Buena Vista.** An old conservative neighborhood with large mansions and converted flats.

3 Alpine/Waller & Duboce. *Sidewalk stairway.*
3 Ashbury Terrace/at No. 64, near Piedmont. *Baker & Haight into Buena Vista Park.*
☆ Buena Vista East/Haight, into Buena Vista Park. *The stair would rate 4 in a more benign location.*
2 Buena Vista East/No. 437, into Buena Vista Park. *Wooden. One of a series of three.*
4 Buena Vista Terrace/Buena Vista East & Duboce into Buena Vista Park. *Ornament above entrance wall gives unusual effect. Curving steps. View.*
☆ Buena Vista West/Haight, into Buena Vista Park. *Lovely. One of the early, beautiful San Francisco neighborhoods—but be careful in your wanderings.*
4 Buena Vista West & Java/into Buena Vista Park. *Wooden.*
☆ Central & Buena Vista West/into Buena Vista Park. *Stone stairway.*
4 Corona Heights Park. *New series of wooden stairs, new plantings by Native Plant Society. Surrounds Randall Junior Museum.*
3 DeForest/Beaver & Flint. *A stairway street, three feet wide and 125 feet long, built around 1975. At the top is Corona Heights Park.*
3 Duboce/Castro & Alpine. *Special. Twenty-five percent grade.*
3 Frederick & Buena Vista West/into Buena Vista Park. *Concrete, wide. Should be extended.*
4 Welland Lathrop Memorial Walk/into Buena Vista Park. *Across from 547 Buena Vista West. Pine trees, view. Lathrop was one of the early modern dance teachers in San Francisco.*
2 Lyon & Haight/into Buena Vista Park.
2 Park Hill & Buena Vista East/into Buena Vista Park. *New stairways are being built in Buena Vista Park.*
4 Waller/Broderick & Buena Vista West. *Sidewalk stairway, easy risers. View of Mt. Diablo.*
☆ Waller/Broderick, into Buena Vista Park. *Garrett Eckbo was the architect of Buena Vista Park erosion control measures which include stairways. Work in progress. Hidden. View.*

■ **Chinatown.** A special combination of sounds, smells, and colors.

2   California/opposite No. 660, into St. Mary's Square. *A relatively low-rated stairway in a fascinating locale.*
3   Clay/Kearny & Grant, into Portsmouth Square.

■ **Diamond Heights.** A neighborhood of views, hills, and canyons.

4   Coralino/No. 289 Amber to No. 92 Cameo. *Woodsy. White-crowned sparrows love it.*
☆   Diamond Heights Blvd./No. 687 28th St.
3   Moffitt at Diamond. *A very necessary stairway corner.*
5   Onique/No. 101 Berkeley—No. 289 Berkeley—No. 400 Gold Mine-Topaz. *Forty-five-degree view of San Francisco. Surroundings of eucalyptus, pine, canyons, hummingbirds. A four-tiered Chinese hopscotch walk.*
2   Opalo/No. 160 Gold Mine to Christopher Park. *Christopher Park is next to Diamond Heights shopping center.*
2   27th St./at No. 881 to No. 5150 Diamond Heights Blvd. *Adjoining Douglass Playground. Part of a long stairway outlined by trees. Nice access.*

■ **Dolores Heights.** A lovely, hilly neighborhood in the Mission.

5   Cumberland/Noe & Sanchez. *Very impressive.*
4   Cumberland/Sanchez & Church. *View. Hidden. Additional curving ramp and wall. Dense vegetation.*
5   Liberty/Noe & Rayburn. *Beautifully designed foliage plantings. Art Moderne houses alongside. View to east and west.*
3   9th St./over MUNI Metro into Dolores Park.
4   Sanchez/19th St.& Cumberland. *City-designed entrance stairway plus sidewalk stairs. At top, four large, 60-year-old cypresses alongside. View.*
5   Sanchez/Liberty & 21st St. *Network of stairs, one of the most beautiful series in the City. View.*
5   20th St. & Noe. *Impressive. Backdrop of high curving wall.*
5   20th St./Sanchez. *Two stairways descending gracefully. Views. Enters a cul-de-sac that connects with Noe stairway and ramp.*

■ **Downtown.** A neighborhood of significance and diversity.

2   Ellis/Market, down to BART/MUNI Metro station. *Rather steep.*
1   Embarcadero/Market, down into BART/MUNI Metro station. *Built in 1973. Concrete stairway and wall, brushed aluminum railings. Interesting new edifices of financial district.*

2   Grant Ave. Gate Stairway at Bush. *Just enough of a lift into another world.*

2   Market/down into BART/MUNI Metro station. *Very steep.*

3   Montgomery/Market, down to BART/MUNI Metro station. *In the financial district among historic and nonhistoric highrises. Bubbled tile wall.*

1   Powell/Geary, into Union Square. *Magicians, music, skits, street artists: lots of local color.*

4   Powell/Market, down to BART/MUNI Metro station. *Wide esplanade into Hallidie Plaza and visitors information center.*

1   Stockton/Geary, into Union Square.

1   Stockton/Post, into Union Square.

2   Stockton/Sutter & Bush. *Over the Stockton Tunnel.*

2   Van Ness/Market, down to MUNI Metro station.

■ **Edgehill.** The steepness of the hill limits the number of homes on this street that winds up to the summit.

3   Edgehill/Kensington—Granville—Allston—Dorchester.

5   Pacheco/Merced & Vasquez. *Echoes the Grand Stairway to the north.*

3   Vasquez/opposite No. 233 Kensington—Merced.

3   Verdun/Claremont—Lennox.

■ **Embarcadero.** Area undergoing rejuvenation and renovation since 1989 earthquake.

5   Commercial/Sansome & No. 1 Embarcadero Center. *Sculpture at entrance; concentric circle of tiles in pavement carry forward the visual pattern throughout the Embarcadero Center & Hyatt Regency Hotel. See sculpture, tapestries, & gardens throughout Center.*

4   Maritime Plaza/Washington/Clay/Battery/Front & Davis. *Six sets of stwys. Open space.*

■ **Eureka Valley.** This neighborhood has a community organization active since 1881, a large gay population, fine Victorians, and the Castro—a movie palace from 1923.

3   Caselli/Clayton & Market.

2   Church Street Footbridge/19th St. over MUNI tracks.

3   Collingwood/20th & 21st Sts. *It helps not to look up.*

1   Douglass/19th. *If someone insists on a stair, you can't stop them.*

4   Douglass/20th St. & Corwin. *Delightful discovery. Trees alongside.*

3   Douglass/Corwin. *Solution to elevating and lowering streets.*

4 Elizabeth/Hoffman & Grand View. *One of the grandest of the sidewalk Stwys.*

2 No. 601 Grandview/24th St. to Market.

2 19th St./No. 4612 & No. 4606 to Caselli.

2 Prosper/16th St.& Pond. *Behind Eureka branch library—an inviting place, a fine book collection.*

2 Romain/Douglass. *Upper to lower levels.*

2 Seward/Douglass & 19th St. *Three sets of stairs. Enriches street by adding another level of viewing. Also very useful.*

3 21st St./Castro & Collingwood.

4 22nd St./Collingwood & Diamond.

3 22nd St./Collingwood & Castro. *Profuse plantings.*

■ **Excelsior.** A stable neighborhood of diverse ethnic groups. Stairways reminiscent of the everyday kind in European towns.

2 Athens/Avalon & Valmar.

2 Campus Lane/Princeton & Burrows.

3 Dwight/Goettingen & Hamilton. *View. Very long.*

2 Excelsior/at No. 1021 into McLaren Park.

3 Excelsior/Munich & Prague.

2 Gladstone/Silver & Oxford.

3 Goettingen and Dwight.

2 Kenney Alley/at No. 646 London to Mission. *Difficult to find.*

4 Munich/Ina & Excelsior. *Hidden. View. One of the newer (1977) stairways in the city.*

3 Munich/McLaren Park & Excelsior.

1 Naglee/Alemany & Cayuga. *Natural headend of Cayuga Creek.*

4 Peru/Athens & Valmar. *Aggregate and railroad ties, designed by R. Schadt. Great views.*

3 Prague/ Munich & Brazil & McLaren Park.

1 Restani/Cayuga & Alemany. *Practical. Hidden—only the residents know it.*

☆ Trumbull/Mission & Craut.

■ **Forest Hill.** The City has recently accepted responsibility for maintaining the non-regulation streets and sidewalks of this neighborhood.

4 Castenada/at No. 140 to No. 334 Pacheco to No. 5 Sotelo. *Adjacent is a Maybeck house with delightful details: carved grapevines along the eaves.*

5 Montalvo/No. 376 Castenada—San Marcos—9th Ave.—Mendosa. *Variety in terrain, architecture, and "custom-made" stairways.*

5   Pacheco/Magellan & No. 249 Castenada. *Grandest and most elegant of all San Francisco stairways.*
4   Alton/Pacheco at No. 400 to No. 60 Ventura.
5   Alton/8th Ave. & No. 20 Ventura.
2   San Marcos/Dorantes. *Rounding a corner.*
5   Santa Rita/at No. 60, to upper Pacheco at No. 349. *View of Marin.*
2   12th Ave./Magellan & Dorantes.

■ **Forest Knolls.** A neighborhood heavily forested with eucalyptus.

4   Ashwood Stairway/Clarendon, No. 95 & No. 101 Warren. *View across to Mt. Davidson. Among the trees.*
4   Blairwood Lane/No. 109 Warren, No. 95 & No. 101 Crestmont. *View. Green railings, which camouflages it among pine and acacia. Floating stairs. Over-realistic view of TV tower.*
3   Glenhaven Lane/Oak Park & No. 191 Christophei.
5   Oakhurst Lane/Warren & Crestmont. *View of ocean. Difficult. Longest continuous stairway to highest elevation in San Francisco. Eucalyptus forest.*

■ **Fort Funston.** Part of Golden Gate National Recreation Area. Off Hwy. 35, south of zoo.

4   "Horsetail" Stwy., left of parking lot, down along Pliocene-age cliffs, to ocean shore. *Plan trip for low tide. Great view of hang gliding activity.*

■ **Glen Park.** Cows roamed the meadowland in this neighborhood in the 1880s.

3   Amatista Lane/Bemis & Everson. *Hardy.*
2   Arlington/at No. 439 to San Jose. *Hidden.*
3   Bemis/Addison & Miguel. Across from #41 Bemis.
2   Burnside/Bosworth.
2   Chilton/Bosworth & Lippard.
2   Cuvier/San Jose & Bosworth.
3   Diamond/Bosworth & Monterey into BART station. *View. Variety of textures in walks and stairs.*
2   Diamond/Moffitt.
2   Hamerton/Bosworth & Mangels.
1   Roanoke/San Jose & Arlington. *A walker's solution to freeway divisiveness.*
1   San Jose/Randall & Bosworth.
1   St. Mary's/San Jose & Arlington.

■ **Golden Gate Heights.** Carl Larsen from Denmark deeded this acreage to the city in 1928.

3   Aerial Way/No. 475 Ortega & No. 801 Pacheco. *Long. Ice plant to stabilize soil. Part of a network of stairways, all rated 4 or 5.*

2   Aloha and Lomita. *Part of a network, all highly rated.*

5   Cascade Walk/Ortega, Pacheco & Funston. *Secluded. Special.*

3   Crestwell/off Ortega.

3   Encinal Walk/14th & 15th Avenues.

4   15th Ave./Kirkham & Lomita. *View.*

4   15th Ave./Kirkham & Lawton. *Pine trees alongside. Walk up slowly.*

4   14th Ave./Pacheco. *Very long trek up.*

4   Lomita/Kirkham & Lawton. *View of houses on stilts.*

4   Mandalay Lane/No. 2001 14th & 15th Aves. & Pacheco. *Ocean view.*

5   Moraga/west from 12th, east from 17th Ave.

4   Mount Lane/No. 1795 14th Ave. No. 1798 15th Ave.

4   Noriega/15th Ave. & Sheldon Terrace. *Huge rock outcropping.*

4   Oriole Way/Pacheco & Cragmont. *Lots of foliage and long landings. View of houses on stilts.*

4   Ortega Way/14th Ave. & No. 1894 15th Ave. *Very long and very practical. Ocean view. Ice plants on sides.*

4   Pacheco/15th Ave. *View.*

2   Pacheco & 14th Ave. *A snippet for rounding a corner.*

4   No. 500 Quintara/14th & 15th Aves. *Great sunset viewing area. Double stairway a third of the way. Built 1928. View.*

3   Quintara at corner of 16th Ave. *Nice curving wide rounded corner.*

5   Selma Way/No. 477 Noriega & No. 564 Ortega. *View. High, high, high.*

3   16th Ave./Kirkham & Lawton. *Stairway built before the surrounding houses.*

3   16th Ave./Pacheco & Quintara. *Series of small stairways. Graceful.*

5   12th Ave./Cragmont, into Golden Gate Heights Park. *Cobblestone stairs.*

■ **Golden Gate Park.** Stairs still being built here.

3   Anglers Lodge/off Kennedy Dr., opposite Buffalo Paddock. *Stone stairway.*

3   Arboretum near Sunset Garden.

3   Children's Playground to Kezar Dr.

3   Conservatory (east of). *Dahlia gardens. Concrete stair.*

3   Fulton & 10th Ave. *Wide railroad tie/blacktop stairs. Into play and rest area. Designed by Walter Kocian.*

3   Fulton & 8th Ave. *Side of DeYoung Museum.*

3   Fulton & Arguello. *Curving railroad tie stairs and sides.*

3   Horseshoe Court. *Built in the 1930s.*

3   Huntington Falls/top of Strawberry Hill to Stow Lake. *Railroad tie-and-chicken wire boxes filled with boulders and stones. A stairway for giants and a giant waterfall.*

2   Japanese Tea Garden to north side of Stow Lake.

2   South Dr. (Martin Luther King Dr.) near Murphy Windmill to Great Highway. *Continues to footpath.*

2   South Dr. (Martin Luther King Dr.) to Big Rec area.

2   South Dr. (Martin Luther King Dr.) to Stow Lake.

3   South Dr. (Marin Luther King Dr.)/intersection at Kennedy Dr. Wooden. *Leads to footpath.*

3   Stow Lake/south side, to south side Strawberry Hill. *Wooden stairs.*

5   Strawberry Hill/from top to Stow Lakeshore. *Fine view. Built of railroad ties, will connect with two new stairways, one on each side of Huntington Falls.*

■ **Ingleside Terrace.**

3   San Leandro/Moncado (No. 344) & Ocean. *44 stairs.*

3   Wyton/Denslowe & 19th Ave. (Footpath/stairway).

■ **Land's End.** Great area for ocean breezes and beach.

4   Eagle's Point/Coastal Trail & the Ocean.

3   Land's End Stwy./lower footpath & Fort Miley parking.

4   Mile Rock/Coastal Trail & the Ocean. *One of the new stairways.*

5   Milestone Stwy./Merrie Way & Sutro Baths. *Railroad tie.*

4   Naval Memorial Stwy./48th Ave. & El Camino del Mar.

5   Sutro Heights Park: 48th Ave./Point Lobos Ave. & Anza. *21-acre estate of Adolph Sutro, purchased in 1881. Stone stwy. to ramparts offers excellent view of ocean.*

■ **Marina.** Development of this neighborhood was given impetus from the 1915 International Exposition.

3   Fort Mason/Bateria San Jose & Picnic areas.

3   Fort Mason/Great Meadow to piers, opposite Bldg. E.

3   Fort Mason/Picnic Area & Tier 3.

4   Fort Mason/upper fort to Aquatic Park. *View.*

4   Jefferson/Beach, Hyde & Larkin.

■ **Mission.** One of the largest districts in San Francisco. Divided into more than a dozen sub-neighborhoods.

3   17th St./Potrero & Bryant, into Franklin Square.
3   16th St./Bryant, into Franklin Square.
3   24th St./Mission, down in BART station.

■ **Mount Davidson.** A neighborhood encircling the highest point in San Francisco.

2   Balboa Park BART station.
2   Balboa Park/San Jose Ave.
3   Bengal/Miraloma & Lansdale. *Wooden risers, concrete and cobblestone steps.*
3   Burlwood/Los Palmos. *Curving a corner.*
4   Dalewood Way, from Mt. Davidson. *Stone and moss stairways through nature trails of pine and eucalyptus.*
4   Detroit/Joost, Monterey & Hearst. *Very handy. A street stairway, crossing a main thoroughfare. Compare with Harry St.*
2   Globe Alley/No. 96 Cresta Vista to Hazelwood near Los Palmos. *Combination easement and stairway.*
2   Lulu Alley/Los Palmos & No. 450—No. 500 Melrose. *Combination easement and stairway.*
4   Melrose/Teresita to Mangels to Sunnyside Playground. *Starts down from No. 195 Melrose. Lots of variety in the stair series. Melrose is a double street! The 800 block Teresita is across from No. 195 Melrose.*
3   Miraloma/Portola. *Goes to pedestrian skyway to West Portal neighborhood.*
3   Myra/No. 95 Coventry & Dalewood. *Hidden. Curved and grooved lane.*
4   Rex/Juanita & Marne. *Fog, moss, stone and fresh air.*
3   Yerba Buena/Ravenwood.

■ **Nob Hill.** A famous neighborhood well-known to tourists.

4   Joice/Pine, Sacramento, Powell & Stockton. *Graceful curve at Pine.*
2   Mason/southeast corner of California.
2   Priest/opposite #1350 Washington, to Clay.
2   Reid/Washington & Clay. Connects to Priest Stwy.
3   Sacramento/Taylor & Mason into Huntington Park
3   Taylor/California & Sacramento into Huntington Park.
4   Taylor/Pine & California. *Sidewalk stairway on both sides of the street, 235 steps.*

■ **Noe Valley.** An authentic neighborhood.

4 Castro/28th & Duncan. *Panoramic views. Franciscan rock formation. Wildlife haven. Strenuous walking.*

3 Castro/Day & No. 590 30th Sts. *We have non-streets and double streets intersecting; now it's stairways meeting. Adjacent Franciscan rock cliffs. Entrance to Glen Park neighborhood.*

5 Cumberland/Noe. *Cobblestone wall. Zigzag contour of stairs. View.*

3 No. 493 Day up to No. 2350 Castro. *Go up.*

3 Diamond/Valley. *Wildlife haven. Great moon-viewing lookout. Panoramic view.*

2 Duncan/Noe toward Sanchez. *Duncan is so steep that it is cut off from traffic at this point and further toward Diamond.*

3 Elizabeth/Hoffman & Grand View.

5 Harry/at No. 190 Beacon to Laidley. *Unusual stairway that connects to Noe Valley, Glen Park—maybe Diamond Heights, too. Very hidden. Built in 1932 by Eaton & Smith, contractors.*

2 Noe/Army & 27th St. *Sidewalk Stairway.*

4 Liberty/Sanchez & Church. *Stairways here. Very inviting area, lots of foliage.*

2 Sanchez/Cumberland.

4 22nd St./Church & Vicksburg. *Sidewalk stairway. If you feel you're sliding backward, it's because the steps slope backward. One of the steepest climbs in the city.*

3 27th St./Castro & Newburg. *Views. Stairway at end of cul-de-sac blocked off.*

2 Valley/Castro to Noe. *Steep driveways show height of original street.*

■ **North Beach.** A neighborhood in transition from predominantly Italian settlers to Chinese.

2 Brenham Place/Washington & Kearny.

4 Jack Early Park. *An oasis for contemplation.*

2 Romolo/Vallejo & Fresno, west of Kearny.

3 Tuscany/Lombard. *Like the Winchester Mystery House stairs: goes nowhere.*

■ **Pacific Heights.** A neighborhood that has maintained standards in architecture and appearance. Enviable views and private schools.

5 Baker/Vallejo & Broadway. *Plantings of Monterey pine, marguerites, hebe. Walk on the west side and experience stair walking vs. uphill walking!*

4   Broderick/Broadway & Vallejo. *One of the few stairways whose designer is known: Schubert & Friedman, 1979. View.*

3   Across from No. 1171 Clay/Washington, Sproul & Taylor.

3   Fillmore/Green & Vallejo. *Stop for extra breath on this sidewalk stairway, presented by the Fillmore Street Improvement Association in 1915.*

3   Gough/Clay, into Lafayette Park. *Near tennis courts.*

3   Gough/Washington, into Lafayette Park.

4   Green/Scott & Pierce. *Stairway imbedded in center of wide sidewalk.*

3   Laguna/Washington, into Lafayette Park. *Sunbathers in summer.*

5   Lyon/Green & Vallejo & Broadway. *Designed by Louis Upton, 1916. View. Complete arrangement of stairs, planting areas, landings.*

4   Normandie Terrace/Vallejo. *Built in 1938, not accepted by the city until 1976.*

3   Octavia/Washington & Jackson. *Surrounded by mansions. Stairways within island of cul-de-sac. Obviously planned, but for what?*

5   Pierce/Clay & Washington, into Alta Plaza. *Beautifully proportioned, extremely wide, tiered. Amid low shrubbery and lawn.*

3   Pierce/Jackson & Washington, into Alta Plaza. *Sunny. View to North Bay.*

3   Sacramento/Laguna & Gough, into Lafayette Park. *Stairway originally went to house of one Holladay, a squatter! Dog run area nearby.*

5   Scott/Clay & Washington, into Alta Plaza. *Elegant stairway surrounded by elaborate Victorians.*

5   Steiner/Clay & Washington, into Alta Plaza. *Beginning a series of off-cornered, off-centered, wide stairs.*

5   Steiner/Washington & Jackson, into Alta Plaza. *Imposing entrance. Benches and paths to four corners of the park.*

3   Vallejo/Scott & Pierce. *Sidewalk stairway.*

3   Webster/Broadway & Vallejo. *Sidewalk stairway across from Flood Mansion, which is now a private school.*

■ **Parnassus Heights.** Home of UC Medical School, with Sutro Forest, once Ishi's preserve, as the background.

3   Farnsworth/Edgewood & Willard. *Beautiful, meandering and shy.*

■ **Portola.** A neighborhood showing strains.

3   Beeman Lane/Wabash & San Bruno.

3   Campbell/San Bruno & Bayshore.

3   San Bruno & Arletta.

3   Sunglow Lane/Gladstone & Silver.

■ **Potrero Hill.** Beautiful weather and views.

3   Army/Evans & Mississippi.

3   Carolina/19th & 20th Sts. *Views of Bay Bridge and freeway network. Embankment plantings by Victoria Mews Assoc. Beautiful. Secluded.*

2   Mariposa/Utah & Potrero. *Sidewalk stairway.*

☆   Missouri/opposite No. 571 near Sierra, to Texas. *Two stairways going nowhere.*

3   22nd St./Arkansas & Wisconsin. *Rural. View.*

2   22nd St./Kansas & Rhode Island. *Sidewalk stairway. Very steep.*

4   Vermont/20th to 22nd Sts. Curly street. *Several stairways radiating from successive cul-de-sacs. Stairway to McKinley Square. Great view.*

■ **Presidio.** Founded in 1776 by the Spanish; Moraga and Anza, leaders.

3   Barnard/Hicks, up to Presidio Blvd. *Exploring area.*

2   Presidio Boulevard/MacArthur Avenue & Letterman Boulevard. *Series of small stairways.*

3   Lincoln Blvd./Pershing Dr. & Cobb Ave. to Bakers Beach. *Logs and chain. Excellent view of Golden Gate.*

■ **Richmond.** Known as the Sand Waste area in early days of San Francisco.

5   California/32nd Ave.& golf course, to Lincoln Park. *Surrounded by cypresses. 29-foot-wide stairway with landings, benches. Footpath around to the Legion of Honor.*

1   El Camino del Mar/Palace of the Legion of Honor. *Come here for the setting, it's unsurpassed. Lots of paths to explore in this national urban park.*

1   48th Ave./Balboa & Sutro Heights. *Magnificent view of wild ocean; take stairs on right-hand side. In front of No. 680 48th, well-worn footpath up to Sutro Heights.*

4   Lake/El Camino del Mar to 30th Ave. *Stairways between three levels of Lake. Very pretty.*

4   Seacliff/from No. 330 toward China Beach. *In the elegant Seacliff neighborhood.*

4   27th Ave./Seacliff & El Camino del Mar. *Beautiful area. Four brick stairways.*

■ **Russian Hill.** Grave of Russians buried on the hill account for the neighborhood name.

5   Broadway/Jones & Taylor. *Very narrow, centered sidewalk stairway.*

5   Chestnut/Polk & Larkin. *In center of Chestnut cul-de-sac. Very wide. Foliage. Double staircase up to Larkin.*

3   Culebra Ter./No. 1256 Lombard & Chestnut. *Charming. Miniature 'village' islet. Terraced.*

5   Filbert/Hyde & Leavenworth. *Sidewalk stairway. Coit Tower straight ahead. 124 steps: a strenuous walk up a 31.5-percent grade.*

3   Florence/Broadway & Vallejo. *Charming. Pueblo Revival houses nearby. 1939 stairway.*

5   Upper Francisco/Upper Leavenworth & Hyde. *Ivy cascading down walls, urns, view to the north, pines.*

4   Green/Jones & Taylor. *Next to No. 940 Green, high-rise almost smack in front.*

5   Greenwich/Hyde & Larkin. *Set into tennis courts.*

5   Greenwich/Hyde & Leavenworth. *View.*

5   Greenwich (south side)/Leavenworth & Jones. *Michelangelo Park. Neighborhood activist, Nan McGuire, spearheaded extraordinary transformation of ugly space into esthetic multi-use park with stwys., plants, tables, benches, community garden, play equipment.*

5   Havens/Leavenworth & Hyde. *Cul-de-sac: entrance only on west side of Leavenworth. Charming.*

2   Himmelman Pl./Mason & Taylor to Broadway. *Utilitarian, with mini park alongside.*

1   Houston/Jones & Columbus. *Next to No. 2430 Jones.*

3   Hyde and Francisco. *Deeply grooved staired corner. Necessary.*

5   Jones/Filbert & Union & Green. *Nicely proportioned. Raised sidewalk stairway. Hard work. Stairs have a visual pattern of horizontal louvered shades.*

4   Larkin/Bay & Francisco. *Long series of stairs. Pass by reservoir paths.*

3   Larkin/Chestnut & Francisco to Bay. *Begins at No. 2745 Larkin. View of reservoir and slope of wild plants.*

4   Leavenworth/Chestnut & Francisco. *Walk on west side to long rampart, try both upper and lower approach.*

5   Lombard/Hyde & Leavenworth. *Curly here, straight there.*

2/5 Macondray Lane/Leavenworth & Jones, Union & Green. *The eastern section of Macondray is Shangri-la, the western is not.*

3   Montclair Terrace/Lombard & Chestnut. *Hidden.*

5   Vallejo/Jones & Taylor. *Retaining wall dates 1914. View. Entrance to special section of Vallejo, and houses designed by Willis Polk on Russian Hill Place. Stairways also designed by Polk.*

5   Vallejo/Mason & Taylor. *Winding.*

2   Valparaiso/Filbert & Greenwich on Taylor.

■ **South of Market**. Once an early residential neighborhood; now industrial.

3   Beale/Main & Fremont to Harrison. *Ed. Beale was the first to bring gold samples to the east coast, 1848. On old Rincon Hill, anchor of the Bay Bridge.*

☆   Lansing/First Street & Essex. *Freeway fumes with every breath: once (in Gold Rush times) this was an elegant neighborhood.*

4   Yerba Buena Gardens/Mission & Howard, 3rd & 4th Sts. *The area, after 30 years of being a civic eyesore, has evolved into the pride of San Francisco. 5 1/2 acre park, galleries, butterfly gardens, outdoor sculptures, 20-foot high waterfall.*

■ **St. Francis Wood**. Architect-designed gates and fountains at boulevard entrance.

3   Junipero Serra/19th Ave.
2   Miraloma/Yerba Buena.
2   Miraloma/Upper Yerba Buena.
3   Portola/Claremont.
3   Portola/Santa Clara. *Across from No. 1420 Portola. West of Vicente. Near Terrace.*
1   Stonestown Stwy./19th Ave. & Stonetown Center. *Across from Mercy High School.*
5   Terrace Walk /San Anselmo & Yerba Buena. *Newly rebuilt of solid redwood, amid trees and park land.*
3   San Anselmo/St. Francis & San Andreas.

▤ **Sunnyside**. Neighborhood worth exploring.

5   Next to No. 233 Joost down to Monterey Blvd., via historic Sunnyside Conservatory. *Unusual landscaping designed by Ted Kipping, neighbor and arborist.*

■ **Telegraph Hill**. Early photos show stairways literally hanging over the cliffs of this history-ridden neighborhood.

2   Bartol Alley/at No. 379 Broadway, to Montgomery & Prescott. *Franciscan formation under an adjacent house.*
4   Calhoun/upper to lower, Union & Montgomery. *View. Unexpected eye-opener.*
3   Child/Lombard & Telegraph Pl. *Almost unseen. Form and function in accord.*
5   Filbert/Grant & Kearny. *Next to Garfield School. Steps of perfect proportion.*

3 Filbert/Kearny.
5 Filbert/Telegraph Hill Blvd., Montgomery & Sansome. *Special, personalized stairway. Wonderful, extensive plantings.*
4 Francisco/Kearny & Grant. *An attractive access to Coit Tower.*
2 Genoa Place/Union, Kearny & Varennes.
4 Greenwich/Grant & Kearny. *An attractive way up to the summit of the hill and Coit Tower.*
5 Greenwich/Telegraph Blvd. & Montgomery & Sansome. *Moving a grand piano to a house on the Greenwich Stairs would be difficult.*
4 Grant/Francisco & Pfeiffer St. Jack Early Park. *An oasis for neighborhood residents and others. Perfect for moon viewing.*
3 Julius Street/Lombard & Whiting. *Not easily seen.*
3 Kearny/Francisco. *Wooden stairs that begin in a garden setting, and end in a gardened cul-de-sac with an unusual elevated walkway in between.*
5 Kearny/Lombard & Telegraph Hill Blvd. *View.*
4 Kearny/Vallejo & Broadway. *Total pedestrian block. Strenuous. Adjacent post-1906 houses are unfortunately disappearing.*
5 Lombard/Kearny & Telegraph Hill Blvd. *View.*
4 Montgomery/Green & Union.
3 Montgomery/Union & Greenwich.
3 Pardee Alley/near Grant to Greenwich.
2 San Antonio Place/Vallejo to Kearny & Grant.
4 Union/Calhoun & east cliff of Telegraph Hill. *Closeup of geologic formation of the hill. View.*
3 Vallejo/Montgomery & Kearny. *Angled and & tiered. Plantings throughout.*

■ **Twin Peaks.** A focal point for the entire city as outlined in the 1905 Burnham Beautification report, forgotten in the mad rush to rebuild after the 1906 earthquake and fire.

2 Burnett/opposite No. 535, upper to lower.
4 Clayton/Corbett. *View. Lovely transitional stairway. Fine specimen of a corner-rounding design.*
3 Clayton/Market. *Graceful corner-rounder.*
3 Copper/Greystone & Corbett, next to No. 301 Greystone & No. 592 Corbett. *Extraordinary view. Stairway in the process of disappearing.*
2 Crestline/at No. 70, to Parkridge. *View.*
2 Cuesta Court to Corbett.
4 Cuesta Court/Portola & Corbett. *Exceptional view. Cotoneaster and Monterey pines.*
4 Dixie/Burnett & Corbett. *Rural. BLOCKED OFF FROM ACCESS.*

2   Fredela Lane/Clairview Court & Fairview Court.

2   Fredela Lane/Lower Marview & Clairview Court.

2   Gardenside/Burnett. *View.*

2   Gardenside/Parkridge. *Glorious views.*

5   Pemberton Place/Crown & Clayton. *View. Shangri-la, 1942- vintage stairway. 1995 redesign and renovation. Stamped concrete stairs, terracotta color; handrails, lights. Designed by Brian Gatter.*

3   Stanyan—near No. 1289. *Up to Belgrave, formerly up to Clarendon.*

■ **Upper Market.** The neighborhood is enjoying a renaissance. Gardens and houses are being renovated by community groups.

4   Ashbury, next to No. 64. *(1911-1912 development).*

2   Church/Market, down into MUNI Metro station. *Terrazzo stairway, ceramic tile walls.*

2   Clifford Terrace/Roosevelt. *Curving the corner.*

4   Corbett/at No. 336. *Behind it is a long alley and stairway.*

1   Corbett/17th St. *The two steps serve the purpose of curving the corner.*

3   Corbin Place/17th St.& Corbett.

3   Danvers/18th St. & Market. *A 1946 stairway.*

3   Douglass/States & 17th St. *Charming, tree-lined cul-de-sac with an assortment of Victorians.*

2   Glendale/Corbett.

3   Grand View/next to No. 600 to Market. *View. Accompaniment to modified skywalk. Well-planted area.*

4   Henry/No. 473 Roosevelt & Castro. *Cul-de-sac. Hidden. A charmer.*

5   Iron Alley/No. 495 Corbett to No. 1499 Clayton and extension to Market & Graystone. *View. Unusual sight from below. Wooden stairs. If you don't suffer from agoraphobia, walk down from Corbett and experience city elevations.*

3   Levant/States & Roosevelt. *High retaining wall covered with vines. Butterflies and chickadees abound in the foliage. Curved street complements stairs.*

3   Lower Terrace/Saturn. *Four short stairways that connect with Saturn/Ord Stwy.*

2   Market/Grand View. *Hidden. Watch out for tree trunks.*

4   Market/Short.

4   Mono/Eagle & Market. *Part of a long twitton.*

3   Monument Way/Mt. Olympus. *View. You're at the geographical center of San Francisco.*

4   Monument Way/Upper Terrace. *View. Neighborly.*

1   Ord Court/at No. 2 to Douglass cul-de-sac. *Surprise.*

3   Ord Street/Storrie & Market down to Ord & 18th St. *Happy muraled wall on No. 176 Ord at end of stairway.*

2   Roosevelt/17th St. *Rounding a corner.*

3   Roosevelt Way/Lower Ter. *Cotoneaster shrubs alongside.*

4   Saturn/Ord & 17th St. *Redesigned by Department of Public Works. Benches, planted areas, curving stwy.*

2   Saturn/Temple & 100 block Saturn. *Three series of four to five steps down to street. Good use of stair idea.*

3   17th St./Clayton & Roosevelt to Upper Ter. *Alongside large apartment buildings. Goes to a concentric circle where the view is fabulous.*

2   17th St./Corbett. *Rounding the corner.*

2   17th. St./Mars. *Rounding a corner.*

2   17th St./Roosevelt. *Rounding a corner.*

3   Stanton/Grand View & Market. *Hidden. Will soon be an archaeological find.*

4   Temple/Corbett & 17th St. Next to No. 4399 17th. *Tiered plantings on both sides of stairs.*

5   Vulcan/Levant & Ord. *Not to be missed. Caring neighbors. Cobblestone terracing.*

■ **Western Addition.** This neighborhood survived the 1906 earthquake and grew and grew until it reached its peak during World War II.

☆   Arbol Lane/Turk & Anza Vista. *A street stairway.*

☆   Fulton/Steiner, into Alamo Square.

☆   Grove/Scott & Steiner, into Alamo Square.

☆   Hayes/Scott & Pierce. *Divided street, several stairways.*

☆   Pierce/Fulton, into Alamo Square.

☆   Sonora Lane/O'Farrell & Terra Vista.

☆   Steiner/Grove & Hayes, into Alamo Square.

INDEX